DEC – – 2014

W9-AGQ-048

The Comparative Guide to WordPress in Libraries

WITHDRAWN Woodridge Public Library

Not to be taken from this room

ALA TechSource purchases fund advocacy, awareness, and accreditation programs for library professionals worldwide.

The Comparative Guide to WordPress in Libraries

A LITA Guide

Amanda L. Goodman

WOODRIDGE PUBLIC LIBRARY
3 PLAZA DRIVE
WOODRIDGE, IL 60517-5014
(630) 964-7899

ALA TechSource

An imprint of the American Library Association

CHICAGO   2014

Amanda L. Goodman is the user experience librarian at Darien Library, a public library in Connecticut. She started using WordPress to manage her online presence in 2008. As an MLIS student, she redesigned the Library and Information Studies website at the University of North Carolina at Greensboro using WordPress. Her interests and work duties include web design, digitization, and teaching technology to others. She writes daily about her professional work at www.godaisies.com.

© 2014 by Amanda L. Goodman. All rights reserved except those which may be granted by Sections 107 and 108 of the Copyright Revision Act of 1976.

Printed in the United States of America

18 17 16 15 14   5 4 3 2 1

Extensive effort has gone into ensuring the reliability of the information in this book; however, the publisher makes no warranty, express or implied, with respect to the material contained herein.

ISBNs: 978-1-55570-968-6 (paper); 978-1-55570-982-2 (PDF); 978-1-55570-984-6 (ePub); 978-1-55570-983-9 (Kindle). For more information on digital formats, visit the ALA Store at alastore.ala.org and select eEditions.

Library of Congress Cataloging-in-Publication Data
Goodman, Amanda L.
    The comparative guide to WordPress in libraries : a LITA guide / Amanda L. Goodman.
    pages   cm. — (LITA guides)
    Includes bibliographical references and index.
    ISBN 978-1-55570-968-6 (pbk.)
    1. Library Web sites—Design. 2. WordPress (Electronic resource) 3. Blogs—Computer programs. 4. Web sites—Authoring programs. 5. Library Web sites—Case studies. I. Title.
    Z674.75.W67G66 2014
    006.7—dc23   2013033610

Book design in Berkeley and Avenir. The WordPress logo on the cover is used with permission from the WordPress Foundation.

♾ This paper meets the requirements of ANSI/NISO Z39.48-1992 (Permanence of Paper).

Contents

Preface

If you're interested in this book, you've probably made the decision that a website is the best way to implement your library project. Congratulations! You have a myriad of choices available from hosting a simple one page site through your Dropbox account to hiring an outside company or using free tools to build your own website. Fortunately, you do not have to build a website from scratch—to do that, to paraphrase the great Carl Sagan, you would first need to invent the Web. Instead, you can rely on the powerful and customizable WordPress for your website development needs.

WordPress is free software that allows you to build a website with no coding experience required. However, a successful website does involve some elbow grease, as you must understand the needs of your users, figure out how to best meet their needs, and then implement a solution that gives them the information or experience they are looking for. WordPress is a tool that can help you make a website, but it needs you to make the site great.

Alongside Polly-Alida Farrington, I have cotaught hundreds of students on how to use WordPress to build library websites. While our six-week courses were focused primarily on getting librarians comfortable with the software, I want to go beyond the simple mechanics of WordPress in this book. Our students were often beginners who were directed to or had discovered a need to build a website for their library. However, the desire for a website does not mean that these students possessed the big-picture view of structuring a site that is useful for the end user. This book is therefore the next step in introducing people like my students in how to create a WordPress website that works. WordPress is built to make web development easy—and with help from the libraries surveyed for this book, anyone can build a website to achieve their library's goals and objectives.

In the first part of this book, you will learn about the WordPress software and some of the competitors. In the second part, you will get an overview of web design and how to use WordPress. The third part of this book illustrates how libraries are utilizing WordPress for their web projects. I describe these profiles as faithfully as I could from survey responses and my observations of their website. If there are any mistakes, they are my own. I attempted to contact international libraries with mixed results. While some library types are cut-and-dried (e.g., school libraries), some library projects can cross multiple dimensions. In organizing the websites, I tried to keep library websites of the same type together; however, I deemed some websites special enough to be better classified in another grouping. Additional library WordPress examples may be summarized at the end of certain chapters. These examples may not have been included in-depth due to a lack of space or because the library was unavailable to complete the survey.

Some libraries used WordPress to build their first online presence, while others used it to revamp their website, and still others for a special project. Each library revealed the details of how their website was produced, describes their patrons, and evaluates how the website has fared since launch via a survey. To conclude each library's section, special features are shared that you can use in building your own website. These libraries serve communities that are too small to have a name or are located in the suburbs of a major city, while others support an entire state. From these libraries' examples, you will be able to build a case for using WordPress for your website thanks to the variety of projects that were achieved using this software.

The versions of the software and websites described in this book are the most up-to-date versions available when this book was sent off to print. WordPress or the websites featured may have changed by the time you are reading this text. I acknowledge these limitations but aim to present a firm foundation that will be useful long after these websites are no longer updated.

This book will not give you the complex skills needed to go out and build all the twenty-one library websites from scratch. You will learn the basics of WordPress and web design. You'll also learn about WordPress's capabilities, which will help you plan for launch and future direction. If you are interested in learning more about the topics covered, an annotated list of suggested readings are included in the appendix for further study.

Now, let's get started with WordPress!

Acknowledgments

When I undertook this endeavor, I was unaware of how writing a book really does take a strong community of support. My Twitter friends have been supportive as I tweeted about #bigproject.

My thanks to my mentors—Dr. Nora Bird, David Gwynn, Lauren Pressley, and Beth Filar Williams—who supported me when I was a graduate student and as a librarian.

Polly-Alida Farrington gave me a priceless gift when she approached me to coteach online WordPress classes with her. I had just graduated, and she reached out at that uncertain time and set my feet on the path that I am on today. Thank you, Polly.

From the roster of those online classes, I sought and found welcome feedback and guidance in developing the survey I sent to libraries. Thank you, Susan Hansen, Stacey Hayman, Valarie Massulik, and Robin Salthouse. I wrote this book for you.

Thanks to my colleagues at Darien Library, who inspire me to work harder and do better. They are shaping who I will become as a professional.

My thanks also to Thomas, who has the saintlike endurance to hear me out every night as I chatter on about my work and my projects. And to Jessica, who has been reading my writing for ten years.

Finally, my sincerest gratitude to everyone who made this manuscript possible at ALA: Rob Christopher (marketing coordinator), Siobhan Drummond (project manager), Jenni Fry (managing editor), Patrick Hogan (senior/acquisitions editor), and Johanna Rosenbohm (copy editor).

—Amanda Goodman

PART 1

Understanding WordPress

Chapter One

An Introduction to WordPress

So, what can WordPress do for you? To start, the key term of this software is *free*. As in, you can either download it to put on your server or you can start a hosted website within minutes, all without digging out your credit card. WordPress is open source software that is free for you to download, customize, and use for your website. Open source software is released under a license that allows the end user—that's you—to continue to develop it without paying fees to the original creator. For WordPress, this means that you are free to download WordPress and tinker with the code to make it fit your project's needs. You can learn more about WordPress's license and the official statement on derivative works on their website.[1]

Second, WordPress is a rather simple web development platform that anyone can use to build and maintain a website. You can create a powerful site without ever poking at any code! Of course, your website will be better suited to your needs and tastes if you do dig around in the back end, but with WordPress you don't have to. In fact, as of summer 2013, there are nearly sixty-nine million WordPress websites in existence.[2] This means thousands upon thousands of users have already built nearly anything you can think of. There are also free modules called plugins to extend what WordPress can do. You can change the appearance of your website as often as you change book displays with thousands of free themes. In practice, though, you probably will not change your site's theme so often. The community that supports WordPress is so strong that you can usually find something to help fulfill your website dreams and not pay a dime for it.

The third reason to consider WordPress is that it makes content management easy. WordPress is a content management system (CMS) that centralizes content creation, publishing, and editing. *Content* means text, images, audio, or video files that you want to publish online. In the past you would have needed to create a new web document in HTML for every single page on your website. If something were to change, such as your site's slogan, you would need to go to *every single page* to change it manually. For a small website this is not entirely unreasonable, but for library websites, this is usually not a sustainable practice. Enter the CMS. To manage content in WordPress, you log in to a web interface where you have access to create new content or even to edit, search, or delete older content. Your website's appearance and functionality is managed by the software, so all your writers need to worry about is creating content—not coding web pages.

All of the above is exciting for a cash-strapped library that may or may not have a dedicated webmaster. (You can create a free website that is easy to develop? Sign me up!)

BENEFITS OF WORDPRESS

Quick to Set Up

Got five minutes? If you are installing WordPress on your server, you can get started in as little as five minutes—as soon as you set up your MySQL database. By having your content stored in a MySQL database, your data can be easily backed up or exported to another system. Then to set up the site, you just need to download the files from WordPress.org, upload them to your server, and click on the install URL. Or you can simply go to WordPress.com to sign up for a website. Enter minimal information such as your desired username, e-mail address, and password, and you have your own WordPress website.

No Coding Skills Necessary

Whether you have never written a line of code or are a seasoned coding guru, WordPress allows you to work in the way you prefer. You can build a complete website without ever looking at the code that runs the website. From downloading a new appearance to adding content, you will never be forced to type code. If you do like to code, you can switch the content editor over to HTML mode and format your post to your exact specifications.

Web Interface

In the past, you may have had a dedicated computer in your library for the webmaster. With WordPress's web interface, you can work on your website from any Internet-enabled device. This may be your desktop, laptop, tablet, or even your smartphone. WordPress makes it easy to administer your website at the location of your choosing.

Content Control

There are a lot of ways to control your content in WordPress. You can easily schedule posts to not publish until a set date, which allows posts to be written ahead of time and be published without additional oversight throughout the month. Do you need to protect content with a password? Just mark off a check box and you suddenly have a members-only content area. Images can also be uploaded and displayed in a variety of layouts. Or if your site is going in a new direction, it is easy to select large amount of content and either unpublish it or delete it as needed.

5

Modular

WordPress is a modular system, designed for the user who is setting up a blog-style website—that is, all the tools are already set and available to publish a blog. However, if a blog is not what you desire, you can download additional components, called plugins, to expand WordPress's functionality. This modular method allows you to add only the specific pieces you need for your website. For example, one website may need a way to RSVP to events, while another site needs complex image galleries. By using WordPress without every function imaginable, your website will not suffer unnecessary "code bloat"—and thus won't be slowed down by supporting features that you will never use.

User Management

Users come in two forms: internal and external. Your internal users are people who are contributing content to your website and/or staff members. WordPress comes with roles and permissions to help you manage your editorial workflow. This way the author who is writing content cannot publish without the editor's permission. (If that feels too constraining, you can download plugins that give you more fine-grain control over what different internal users can do.) Similarly, WordPress comes with great support to help you deal with your external users—those who read and comment on your website. You can allow anyone to respond to posts, blacklist words unacceptable to your community, and more, all without you needing to approve each comment.

Appearance

Web designers may be a dime a dozen, but your library may not have one on staff. Instead of taking the time to learn how to design WordPress, you can download a new theme to change the appearance of your website. Finding, installing, and activating a new theme is very simple. Your staff time can then be spent tweaking the theme to customize it to your needs instead of starting from scratch.

Large and Supportive Community

As previously mentioned, WordPress powers millions of websites. The community releases thousands of free themes and plugins each year to help make WordPress your own no matter your project type. If you get stumped, you can find support on WordPress's support forums. Users also document their achievements, developments, and struggles on their own personal websites, so make sure to look outside of the official online community as well.

DRAWBACKS OF WORDPRESS

WordPress is great at what it does. However, as with any web solution, it cannot be everything to everybody. It shares problems common to all CMSs; for example, creating a theme from scratch can be complicated, as you need to learn the specific quirks of this platform. Second, WordPress's most basic purpose is to run blog-style websites. (A blog is a website where content is posted in chronological order, with the focus being strictly on the writer's thoughts or interests. These sites share similar visual characteristics, including a long list of posts that can be navigated forward and backward chronologically. Blogs are usually simple in design, structure, and features. Nonblog websites are usually the opposite: more complex in appearance and utility.) In recent years, WordPress has been building in features to allow greater customization, but more sophisticated systems will take a lot of work to implement.

Advanced Customization Requirements

While coding knowledge is not necessary to build a great WordPress website, you will inevitably run into a problem that requires you to work with PHP. While the official online handbook and community offer lots of sample code for you to copy and paste into your installation, you will often need to tweak the code. For example, on a complex home page, you may want to show only the latest event-related post. You will need to dig into the files that run WordPress to add this function.

Difficulty When Building Very Complex Websites

While WordPress has made it easier to make more complex websites in recent years, the platform is still behind a much more customizable CMS such as Drupal.[3] For example, it is difficult—if not impossible—to aggregate content in different displays based upon specific conditions. Say you have posts about different children's events that contain information about the age groups, date, location, and so on for each event. In Drupal, it would be easy to make this information sortable based on a single characteristic (e.g., age group). This is not a built-in feature of WordPress, so you would have to use complex plugins or code to do the same task as of this writing. You could invest a lot of time to reconfigure WordPress to achieve these goals, but if your website needs very complex interactions, you may wish to investigate other options.

7

Accessibility Issues

Websites are used by people with a variety of abilities and difficulties. WordPress is working on improving their accessibility to all users. One issue noted by librarian and accessibility advocate Holly Mabry is that she has to "enlarge the [WordPress] admin to navigate and write posts/pages, and it crowds everything, or cuts it off."[4]

More to Sort Through When Something Breaks

When you are running a traditional HTML and CSS website, if something breaks it is easier to track down the issue and fix it if you know a little about coding. With WordPress and other CMSs, if something breaks, you have to sort through PHP files, perhaps log in to the database to correct an error, or worry about plugins breaking your website. (Fortunately, if your website has trouble after you install a new plugin, you can usually fix the problem by deleting the plugin from your website's server.)

More Attention from Hackers

Similar to how the Windows operating system is targeted by viruses and malware because of its popularity, WordPress is in the same situation thanks to hackers and spammers. Many people keep the default URL of their log-in page and then use very common usernames such as *admin*, which makes it easier for their site to be hacked. WordPress fights back with frequent updates to fix any bugs and vulnerabilities in their code. Updating the software is painless to do because it is just a button-click away to a safer system. As the webmaster, you can avoid many attacks just by keeping your software updated, keeping your passwords strong, and always thoroughly reading the documentation and forums of new plugins and themes before you install them.

NOTES

1. WordPress.org, "The WordPress License," http://wordpress.org/about/license/.

2. WordPress.com, "WordPress Sites in the World," http://en.wordpress.com/stats/.

3. Drupal, http://drupal.org.

4. Holly Mabry, Twitter post, November 18, 2012, 7:48 p.m., https://twitter.com/hfmabry/status/270327748621369344.

Chapter Two

Flavors of WordPress

WordPress is one of the most flexible content management systems available. You can sign up for an online website to get started immediately, download the software and host your own website, or even launch an entire community of WordPress websites yourself. Polly-Alida Farrington, my coteacher for WordPress classes, and the software creators refers to these different types of WordPress websites as *flavors,* a term that I will borrow for this book. Which flavor of WordPress you use will depend on your technical capabilities and limitations.

The following introductions to each flavor of WordPress will give you an overview of what you can expect from each type, how to get started, and what technical capabilities you will need to implement the software. Keep in mind that the versions of software listed in this book are current to when this book was sent for publication.

WORDPRESS.COM

If you want to dive in and get a taste of the power and ease of WordPress, this is where to start. You can go to WordPress.com and sign up right away. After checking your e-mail and clicking the activation link, you can start building your free WordPress website. The main advantages of using a hosted version of WordPress are that it requires no technical knowledge and you can easily set up your website in no time. However, there are some drawbacks like the limited customization and functionality.

Advantages

- Free
- Immediately available upon signup and activation
- Offers over two hundred professional themes
- Automatically handles maintenance, updates, and site backups
- Large and active WordPress.com community, which gains your website extra traffic

For the most part, your website's administrative interface looks identical to the version you download and host yourself. Many of the great professional themes for WordPress are available only for WordPress.com users. As well, a lot of the stress of running a website is handled entirely by WordPress.com so you can focus on just website creation instead of all the technical stuff.

Disadvantages

- No plugins
- Limited website capabilities compared to a self-hosted version

For someone used to controlling all aspects of their website, the fact that I could not add plugins to my WordPress.com website was a deal breaker for me. However, I have introduced many patrons to WordPress.com who love it and use it for their personal websites. There are hundreds of libraries that use WordPress.com to reach out to their patrons, so the limitations of a hosted site have not stopped others from having a successful web presence.

Customizations

If you want a non-WordPress.com URL, customize a preexisting WordPress.com theme, or the ability to upload lots of media, you can have these features—for a price. These prices are similar to the cheapest web-hosting service providers out there. The difference is that WordPress.com takes care of protecting and backing up your website, while a self-hosted version gives you the ability to completely customize your site. The prices below are current for fall 2012.

- Use your own domain (URL), which costs between $18 and $33 per year. This offers limited customization.[1]

- If you want to further customize your website, it is $30 a year.[2]
- Purchase up to 200GB of storage space for your uploaded media content which costs between $20 and $290 per year.[3]

WORDPRESS.ORG

If you want to have complete control of your website, you will need to host your own WordPress installation. Your server may be run by your library or local municipality, or server space can be purchased through a large host provider such as DreamHost, Bluehost, or HostGator (to name just a few). By hosting WordPress yourself instead of through WordPress.com, you have the ability to customize everything from your site's appearance to its functionality.

To install WordPress on your own server, you need PHP version 5.2.4 or higher and MySQL version 5.0 or higher. Make sure to check the latest requirements before you start.[4] If you are purchasing shared space, make sure that you choose a Linux server instead of a Windows server, as WordPress is easier to install.

11

Advantages

- Free to download
- Gives complete control of your website, from appearance to functionality
- Simple updating of the site's software, themes, and plugins
- Plugins capability

WordPress is easy to install if you have any familiarity with using FTP, editing files, and creating a MySQL database. WordPress boasts that you can install a site in five minutes—which is true once you get the hang of it, but the first time it may take a little longer as you read through the documentation. Detailed information about installing WordPress is available online.[5]

You can also install WordPress on your own computer. A local installation will allow you to get familiar with using themes and plugins unlike the hosted WordPress.com. WordPress lists some resources to help you get started testing the software before you make this commitment.[6] These resources can be as simple as installing a program or as advanced as setting up your own server environment, then installing WordPress.

Disadvantages

- Requires your own server to install the software
- Requires the ability to set up the database

Keep in mind that if you use a cheap shared-hosting service, you have no guarantee that your site will be fast, as your site is competing with hundreds of other websites for the same resources. Also, if your website is suddenly very popular, it runs the risk of being shut down by your server provider for using too much bandwidth. On the other hand, you could purchase a dedicated or virtual private server (VPS), which gives you absolute control over your server. However, this option is considerably more expensive, by hundreds of dollars. If possible, I suggest running your own web servers in-house.

Customizations

The sky is the limit! You can do anything you want. You have complete control over the appearance of your website and how it functions, or if you have the inclination, try your hand at making your own verision of popular websites like Twitter or Facebook. With the time and coding experience, you can customize WordPress to do whatever you want.

WORDPRESS MULTISITE

In 2010, WordPress merged together two separate services: WordPress Multi-User (MU) and WordPress.[7] This change centralized WordPress's codebase, but the winner here is the network maintainer. Now you can run multiple WordPress websites from one installation. This also means that you need only to maintain and update the core WordPress files only once instead of updating each site separately. You can learn more online about how to enable this feature.[8]

Advantages

- One installation for multiple websites
- Creates a network of websites, which allows users to sign up to create their own sites (or you can assign them)

- Control and choice regarding which plugins and themes to install
- Content can be aggregated from all the websites in the network to display on the main site.[9]

In researching this book, the only examples I found of libraries running multisites were academic libraries. These multisites were built to easily enable students and teachers to have a website hosted by the university. By running a network of websites, libraries are able to encourage and cultivate a rich field of content as generated by their community. Another idea is for a library to host local community websites. WordPress Multisite makes it easy for you to provide an unusual but often needed service in your community without a lot of overhead.

Disadvantages

- Many cheap servers will not allow multisites.
- Multisites are more complicated to set up than standard WordPress installation.
- Each individual website may have domain mapping issues.

If you are running websites for a lot of people, expect to hear from them! As a website manager, you will get to hear complaints, requests for new plugins and themes, and so much more. If your library has the resources to support this sort of community, it is a great asset, but you will have to set aside time for responding to your users' questions.

Customizations

- Individual websites cannot install their own plugins or themes.
- Themes and plugins are activated on a network or individual site basis.[10]
- Users can use only plugins and themes that have been approved and activated for them by the network administrator.

Users are limited to customizing their websites based upon the administrator's settings. While this is great for the network maintainer, you will need to make it clear to users how exactly they can customize before they get started.

BE INSPIRED

If you want to see what others have done with WordPress, check out some of the sites below. Note: Most websites you find are probably self-hosted instead of using WordPress.com because you have more flexibility with customizations.

Showcase

http://wordpress.org/showcase/

Showcase is run by the official WordPress website. Anyone can submit a website for consideration for the showcase, but only the best are selected for display. You can browse by tag, flavor, or keyword. Displayed sites include a screen shot, the flavor, tags, a short description, user star ratings, and an explanation of why the website is in the Showcase.

We Love WP

http://welovewp.com/

Each site featured on We Love WP includes a large screen shot, how many people love it, the date the site was posted, how many views it has received, a link to the website, a description, and tags that describe how the site was built or its design type (e.g., "clean"). You can also sort websites by category. Unlike the other two sites here, visitors can leave comments on each site's design.

WP Inspiration

http://wpinspiration.com/

WP Inspiration displays screen shots of a website's home page. When you click on a thumbnail, you are taken to the actual website. You can filter websites by category (e.g. corporate, education, photography) or browse by dominant color of the website.

NOTES

1. WordPress.com, "Domains," http://en.support.wordpress.com/domains/.

2. WordPress.com, "Custom Design: Custom CSS," http://en.support.wordpress.com/custom-design/custom-css/.

3. Wordpress.com, "Space Upgrade," http://en.support.wordpress.com/space-upgrade/.

4. WordPress.org, "Requirements," http://wordpress.org/about/requirements/.

5. WordPress.org, "Installing WordPress," http://codex.wordpress.org/Installing_WordPress.

6. WordPress.org, "Installing WordPress on your own Computer," http://codex.wordpress.org/Installing_WordPress#Installing_WordPress_on_your_own_Computer.

7. WordPress.org, "Version 3.0," http://codex.wordpress.org/Version_3.0.

8. WordPress.org, "Create a Network," http://codex.wordpress.org/Create_A_Network.

9. For example, see Teach for America's Teach for Us, http://teachforus.org/.

10. Brian Casel, "The Beginner's Guide to WordPress Multisite," http://mashable.com/2012/07/26/beginner-guide-wordpress-multisite/.

Chapter Three

The Competition

You have many options when choosing which platform to build your website on. While this section covers Drupal, Omeka, and LibGuides, be sure to look into other software before you invest your time into a platform that will not meet your needs. The three programs discussed here are ones that I have experience in. Other options include Joomla, Weebly, and wiki software such as MediaWiki.[1] Each program has its advantages and disadvantages for a library's website project. If you have the staff, experience, and time, your library could also build its own CMS.

DRUPAL

Another popular open source CMS is Drupal, which also gives you the tools to quickly set up a website—with a catch. While the basics of WordPress can be taught in a couple hours, Drupal has a much steeper learning curve. Drupal was released to the public in 2001, two years before WordPress. However, Drupal did not really start to catch on until 2005.[2] The next major version, Drupal 8, is expected to be released by June 2014.

Comparison to WordPress

WordPress comes out of the box with everything you need to set up a basic website. Drupal has been called a content management framework instead of a CMS.[3] What this means is that while Drupal is very powerful, flexible, and customizable, it does require a lot of back-end configuration just to get your site to a comparable place to the default WordPress setup. On the other hand, you can make a much more complicated website using Drupal.

The good news is that once you have put in the extensive amount of time to learn Drupal, you can build other Drupal websites quickly. There are also efforts to create a more streamline system through the use of Drupal Distributions.[4] A distribution includes everything you need to quickly set up a Drupal website to meet for particular cases. Sample site setups are geared toward publishing, commerce, academic or even church websites.

Hosted Version

However, there is also a hosted version called Drupal Gardens, which is similar to WordPress.com.[5] Drupal Gardens offers a range of pricing levels from free to enterprise (which are for very large organizations such as a news organization or corporation). The point of this hosted version is to take a lot of the hassle of setting up, managing, and hosting your website out of your hands so you can concentrate on content. Drupal Gardens should be thought of as "Drupal as a service."[6] However, despite the advantages offered, you will not be able to extend the functionality of your website by uploading any of the thousands of modules released by the Drupal community.

Self-Hosted Version

If you want to have access to creating a website that has only the exact functionality and appearance that you need—such as WordPress—you will want to host your own version of Drupal. While the installation process is very similar to WordPress, it is the setting up of basic components of your website that can take a lot longer. Therefore, it is especially important to spend a lot of time planning all the functionality of your website before you begin building in Drupal.

For More Information

- Ken Varnum's *Drupal in Libraries* (ALA TechSource/Neal-Schuman, 2012)
- Johan Falk's *Drupal 7: The Essentials* (CreateSpace Independent Publishing Platform, 2011; also available online[7])

- Tom Geller's *Drupal 7: Visual QuickStart Guide* (Peachpit Press, 2010)
- Robert J. Townsend and Stephanie Pakrul's *Foundation Drupal 7* (Friends of ED, 2010)

OMEKA

The newest CMS in this section, Omeka, was created by the Roy Rosenzweig Center for History and New Media at George Mason University.[8] It is an online publishing platform that is aimed at and is gaining momentum within the library, museums, and archives community. Omeka also serves scholars and students who are trying to organize and display their research in an attractive and feature-rich manner. While Omeka could be used as nonarchival software, it is intended to be used for the digital display of items as images. Items are described and can then be displayed and interacted with in a number of different ways through plugins.

19

Comparison to WordPress

Omeka also touts a simple five-minute installation, as with WordPress, and also offers similar user-submitted themes and plugins. The key selling points of Omeka are that it makes it easy to use Dublin Core as the metadata scheme to describe your objects and that it is very friendly for building online exhibits. Since Omeka is especially designed for curated content, your metadata is easy to maintain, update, and display throughout your website. Data migration tools are also baked right into Omeka, so you can do CSV imports and OAI-PMH harvests to share your content with other websites

The WordPress community has contributed several plugins to make more feature-rich installations similar to Omeka:

- Dublin Core for WordPress
  http://wordpress.org/extend/plugins/dublin-core-metadata/
- CSV Importer
  http://wordpress.org/extend/plugins/csv-importer/
- Cropnote
  http://wordpress.org/extend/plugins/cropnote/
- Scripto
  http://wordpress.org/extend/plugins/groupdocs-documents-annotation/

- WP SIMILE Timeline
  http://wordpress.org/extend/plugins/wp-simile-timeline/

You can read more about these plugins in appendix C.

Overall, Omeka is very similar to WordPress in its functionality. The CMS is very popular in academic circles and is well documented through video tutorials.[9]

Hosted Version

Omeka.net is the hosted version of Omeka. Similar to WordPress, you can easily sign up for a free account (which has 500 MB of storage, compared to WordPress. com's 3GB of storage). Hosted websites have access to the Library of Congress's "list of authorities and controlled vocabularies."[10] The number of plugins, themes, and websites you can install depends upon the level of the paid plan. Uploaded items are organized into collections, can be found via tags and keywords, are added to maps, and are put into online exhibits.

Self-Hosted Version

The install for Omeka is almost identical to Drupal and WordPress. You can also install an unlimited number of plugins and themes to build a more complex website. However, unlike the hosted version of Omeka, you are allowed only one site per installation.[11]

More Information

- Check the Use Case studies
  http://info.omeka.net/about/
- Using Omeka to Build Digital Collections: The METRO Case Study
  http://metroblogs.typepad.com/ditrw/2011/04/using-omeka-to-build
  -digital-collections-the-metro-case-study.html

LIBGUIDES

While WordPress and the other competitors listed in this section are open source products, LibGuides is an annually paid service from Springshare. LibGuides is popular among libraries for their online needs.[12] While it is often used as an extension to a preexisting website, LibGuides can also be used as a library's website.

Comparison to WordPress

Unlike WordPress, LibGuides is a paid service whose pricing depends upon the size of your user community.[13] You sign a contract with Springshare, who then sets up your LibGuides on their own servers. When the service goes live, your administrator will need to create all your other user accounts so that staff can start creating subject guides or the pages of your website. LibGuide websites tend to have a very similar appearance, so you must make your own customizations for a unique look. This means writing HTML and CSS code and either copying it into LibGuide's code boxes or linking to your own hosted stylesheets. You can also create reusable templates to help manage the appearance of your guides. Sidebar blocks are also reusable, so once you set up a master template, you can easily replicate it.

Other features similar to WordPress are that you can enable comments for patron feedback, and your text editor looks like a standard document editor (e.g., Microsoft Office). Adding multiple content writers is also handled in a similar fashion.

More Information

- Libraries Using LibGuides
  http://libguides.com/community.php?m=i&ref=www.libguides.com
- Guide FAQ
  http://guidefaq.com/
- LibGuides Help & Documentation
  http://help.springshare.com/index.php?gid=179

NOTES

1. Joomla, www.joomla.org; Weebly, www.weebly.com; MediaWiki, www.mediawiki.org/wiki/MediaWiki.
2. Drupal, "About Drupal," http://drupal.org/about.
3. Larry Garfield, "Drupal Is Not a CMS," Palantir, July 10, 2012, http://palantir.net/blog/drupal-not-cms.
4. Drupal, "Download and Extended," http://drupal.org/project/distributions.

5. Drupal Gardens, www.drupalgardens.com.

6. Dries Buytaert, "Drupal Gardens," Acquia, September 2, 2009, www.acquia.com/blog/drupal-gardens.

7. *Drupal 7: The Essentials* by Johan Falk is available for open source editing: https://drupal.org/node/1576418.

8. Omeka, http://omeka.org.

9. Vimeo, "Omeka's Videos," http://vimeo.com/omeka/videos.

10. Omeka, "Library of Congress Suggest," http://info.omeka.net/build-a-website/manage-themes-and-plugins/library-of-congress-suggest/.

11. Omeka, "What Is Omeka.net?" http://info.omeka.net/about/.

12. Springshare, "LibGuides," http://springshare.com/libguides/.

13. Springshare, "Why LibGuides? The Benefits of LibGuides Web 2.0 Platform," www.springshare.com/libguides/benefits.html.

2

PART 2

The Basics of Developing a WordPress Website

Chapter Four

Website Planning

Website building is a complex endeavor and may be considered a new literacy skill for twenty-first-century learners. For example, fourteen-year-old students in the Henrico County Public Schools build online portfolios to track their learning outcomes as they progress through a school to work program.[1] Likewise, some degree programs also have students submit online portfolios as part of their graduation requirements. In time, this way of sharing learning outcomes may trickle down to secondary school. For those who did not attack web development in school, we can use tools such as WordPress. The process of website creation is removed from the exclusive domain of those who have time to learn lots of coding and programming into the realm of the busy professional.

I have written this section with the students from my online WordPress classes in mind. From the class forums I learned that many students had been told to build a website, but they did not know where to start. Therefore the following section is written for those new to web development, so it is safe to skip over if you are an experienced web developer.

Each section will guide you through the basics of planning a website. Since each topic can cover a book on its own, each section will be short, but you can find additional resources in appendix B to help you on your way. I suggest keeping tracking of your website design process through such services as Google Drive or Trello, a personal favorite.[2] By using these cloud services, you can easily share your work with others and track changes over time. (A cloud service is where your information is stored on a server, which is then accessible from any Internet-capable and -connected device.)

As we saw previously, you can get started with WordPress immediately by heading over to WordPress.com. I encourage you to get familiar with WordPress as soon as possible, but your website will be all the richer if you plan your site first. The more time you spend up front thinking about and planning your website, the better your site will be once it launches. You will know what you want to accomplish, who your audience is, and what metrics to set to measure the success of your website venture. Using this knowledge, you can plan out a website that meets each of your stated goals in a way that patrons can easily find the information and utilize their new knowledge in a way that is useful for them.

This section will assume that you are building the main website presence for your library in your current project. However, when we look at specific usages of WordPress by libraries, you will also find examples of project websites.

DEVELOPMENT AND PRODUCTION SERVERS

At all times you should have two websites for your project. One is the development site where you try out your ideas, test new plugins, and make design decisions before you roll them over to the actual website. This second website is known as the production website. It is live and is what others see when they visit your URL. By testing on your development site, you can discover mistakes or incompatibilities before you publish them on your live site.

In my own work, I do a lot of experimenting on the development website. Eventually this development website looks vastly different than the site the public visits. It is then necessary to wipe the development server and copy the production website back to it so I am back to two identical sites. Before making any major redesign decisions or changes, make sure that your development server is identical again to your production website. You will need to have your entire website—from the database to the plugins—backed up before making any drastic changes.

YOUR GOALS FOR BUILDING A WEBSITE

At this point, you know you need a website, but do you know what you are seeking to accomplish? This question, of course, is based on the type of website you are building: creating your library's very first website, revamping an older website, or building a specific project website. Below are some common goals to consider for these three types.

Creating Your Library's First Website

In the digital age, your library should have already claimed its name space on the web. This may be as simple as a free WordPress.com website that lists the bare minimum details about your library. Or this could be as complex as getting your catalog online and adding interactive elements, such as contact forms and comments. Whatever the case may be, you are on your way to being accessible to your community online.

Goals:

- Set up a home base where patrons can find information about your library. Remember, if you are not online, people may assume you do not exist outside of the white pages.
- Add information about your library's hours and location, and how to get in contact.
- Decide if this website will be updated regularly with building closings, events, and so on, or if it is a build-it-and-forget-it type of website.

Revamping an Existing Website

This website project may be the most difficult of the three! Your library already has an established persona. Staff and patrons alike already have set ideas about what the website looks like and how it is organized. When establishing goals, you may need to take into consideration the current expectations and then work to show how a new site can better meet your library's goals.

Goals:

- Create a website that has a modern visual design.
- Weed out irrelevant or out-of-date content.
- Establish or strengthen existing navigational schemes.
- Consider adding interactive elements such as commenting, social media, or forms.

Building a Project Website

Sometimes an ambitious, specific project—such as a community digital archive—requires its own website. Your project website may be fully integrated with your regular website so that patrons do not realize they are moving from one to another. Or your project website may be a collaborative effort from several individual groups, so your site is not too heavily branded with any one organization's presence.

Goals:

- Decide whether your project will be continuously maintained or just set up and then never updated.
- Establish who your audience is and then write copy appropriate to their reading comprehension level.

AUDIENCE

28

The very first thing you should think about when beginning a project is if a website is what you really need. Once you have established that yes, you need a website, then the second thing is to think about your primary audience. Everything you will do from here on out will be structured around your users' needs. How familiar is your audience with the Web? Do they know conventions such as clicking on the site's logo usually takes them back to the home page? Are they physically capable of using a mouse? If you are building a website for a retirement home, bump your font size up so the text will be easier to read. Below are some aspects of your audience to think about.

> **What would a user want from your website?** While you are dreaming of designing a website filled with engaging content that keeps visitors coming back for more, you should first stop and ask yourself, Why is the user here? What are they trying to accomplish? For library websites, the user is usually online to search your catalog (and then, if your site can handle it, to place a holds request on the item). At this point, make some educated guesses about your audience and what they will want to do on your website. Next, set up some user experience (UX) testing to find out

what it is that your actual targeted audience wants! (We will look at UX later in this section.)

How will your audience access this website? Do your users access the Internet through a mobile device (tablet, netbook, or phone) or through a desktop computer? Mobile users often have download limits (yes, visiting web pages counts as downloading) on their devices that they must adhere to or face unexpected higher phone bills. Their screens are also much smaller than desktop monitors so content needs to be viewable on a smaller device. (Other considerations of mobile users will be visited in the "Mobile Websites" section.) Most desktop users in the United States have high upper limits or no limit on how much they can download on the Internet per month. However, if many in your community are still accessing the Internet through dial-up, you need to be careful about how "heavy" your website is in terms of how long it takes the site to load.

What operating system is on your users' computers? There are also considerations for people who are using a PC or a Mac. Your website may look slightly different using different operating systems due to how the browsers render elements on the web page. The most noticeable for example would be on a download page on your website. For a PC, you would say "right click the link" while on a Mac, the user may hold down the Control key on their computer first before clicking. This does not even begin to cover people who may be using less popular operating systems. If you are building your library's first website, you may not even have the answers to any of these questions. To find out, schedule some time to ask your patrons about how they access the Internet from home. If your library already has a web presence, you can find out in-depth information about the devices your patrons are using by looking at your website analytics. (We will look more at analytics at the end of this chapter.)

What are the technical capabilities of your audience? Your users may be unfamiliar with how to use a computer, let alone the Internet! The interactions and basic knowledge of how to navigate the Web can be daunting for someone just logging on for the first time. Patrons may not know how to open a browser—or that they even need to—or how to find

29

websites online. While your audience is probably diverse with a broad range of experience and tech savviness, try to find ways to make your site easy to use even for someone unfamiliar with how the Web works. However, you also cannot design a website that will meet 100 percent of every single user's needs and understanding of the Web, you can try to reach as many people as possible for your community.

What terminology does your audience understand? Librarians and UX specialists could spend hours arguing the virtues of one term over another. Do you say *reference or research?* Or how about another term entirely, such as *information services?* On your website, you will want to avoid using library jargon in most cases. For example, use the term *magazine or journal* instead of periodical. An even sneakier term is *catalog.* Young people using library websites often see the term *catalog* and have figured out to click on that term to look for materials, but do they know where the term originates? Your best bet in these matters is to do a little user testing to find out which word is best.

What are the physical capabilities and limitations of your audience? While most of your users may be physically capable of using a mouse and keyboard with no visual impairments, there will be patrons who have trouble using a computer due to physical obstacles. For example, if most of your users are on mobile devices but are also older, relying heavily on multitouch navigation may make your website difficult to use.[3] Such users may not be capable of pinching and zooming around the screen. Or if your library serves a school for the blind, your website should be usable by those who are visually impaired. There are even more accessibility issues which we will also overview in that section.

TIME INVESTMENT

How long it takes to prepare and build a website differs from project to project. It is often easier to build a new website than to completely revamp an existing one. Your own technical limitations may also come into play when you have to learn how to use new tools in order to build your website. Fortunately, WordPress is very easy to get off the ground with. However, keep in mind that just because you can publish content immediately does not mean that you should not take the time to plan out your website.

Once your website is live, you need to continue to maintain the content, unless your project is meant to remain static after publication. However, I am going to assume that you are building a website that will continue to grow and develop—or at the very least, you will continue to keep the contact information updated.

How much time is spent on keeping a website updated? It depends on how much content you want to publicize online. For the purpose of the following examples, I am going to assume you are thinking about your library's main online presence. As of June 2012, 90 percent of the United States is online in some form.[4] Since your patrons are likely to be online already, they will want to know the following about your library:

- When is the library open?
- How do I contact the library for more information (e.g., telephone, e-mail, instant messenger)?
- How do I access library resources (e.g., databases, the OPAC, how to obtain a library card)?

The above questions can be considered static content that you do not need to update frequently. You can write up this content before you launch and then not think about it again unless something changes. The key here is that *someone* will need to be in charge of remembering to update the website as things change. Ideally, this person will also be the one with the know-how and log-in credentials to make the needed changes.

Since your website is probably the main way your patrons will learn about your library, your patrons are also interested in what is going on at your library. When are your story times? Do you have any meet-and-greets with authors? If you post information about upcoming events on your website, your time investment in the website increases exponentially over a website that is built and then left to sit. Information about upcoming events can be added daily, weekly, monthly, or quarterly. If your website is well-thought-out beforehand, adding new content is easier because it is obvious where new content should be posted. The important thing to remember is to keep a steady flow of information so patrons know your site is being actively maintained.

YOUR TECHNICAL CAPABILITIES

Like an end-of-year math test, technology skills are a result of cumulative knowledge and experience. If you do not know how to use a computer, you will find it very difficult to build a website. This is not to say that you cannot learn new skills, but it will take longer to launch a fully customized website because you have more things to learn from this starting point than someone who has been using the Internet daily. Fortunately, if you are just getting started and your project is not overly complex, you can try out a hosted WordPress.com website. Besides your own personal technical knowledge, you should consider what is possible through your IT.

Questions to consider:

- Do you need to obtain permission to use WordPress (e.g., from IT, your campus webmaster, your town government)?
- Do you have a local server, or do you need to purchase server space?
- Do you have the budget to host an installed version of WordPress?
- Do you have the software required for an installed version?[5]
    o MySQL database
    o PHP
    o Mod_rewrite Apache module

USER EXPERIENCE (UX) TESTING

When you build a website, you have to think of the needs of many users. Your users for a public-facing website will be both your staff who are providing the content and your patrons who are navigating the site. The interests of different users may compete with one another. Each person also approaches your website with expectations based on their previous experiences with other websites. When you do user testing, you can expect to hear critiques and comparisons to Amazon or Google when you talk about search results.

How you do user testing depends on your financial and time budgets. In larger institutions, you may have access to a usability expert or have the funding to hire one to run user experience (UX) tests for you. However, anyone can do basic UX testing no matter their funding level. The most important aspect is to recruit users and then observe their actions.

UX Tips

- Observe people's behavior as they interact with your website.
- Listen for what is being said—and watch for what is not being said. Your user may be unconscious of their own behaviors or their own particular insights as they navigate your website. For instance, a mother may make an educated guess that information pertaining to children's events should be on the kids' section of your website. A childless patron may believe this information would be on a general library events page.
- Ask about each user's technical knowledge background so you know if you are working with someone who cannot use a mouse versus a power user who is very familiar with the Web. Either extreme can skew your results.
- Ideally, have a second person take notes of the user's actions so you can concentrate on guiding the user through the tests.
- A rule of thumb is that five testers will sniff out most of the usability issues.
- Ask people to think aloud as they go through your usability test.
- Be task focused. Ask people to accomplish specific things on your website, such as finding a story time.
- Focus groups are great for gathering feedback about how people feel about a topic. Try to use focus groups then to ask questions about branding, visuals, and the like.
- If you are having trouble with your site's navigation and how to word things, you can ask people to write down what they would call things (e.g., *news* versus *events*) and then arrange the cards into categories for your website.

Check appendix B for more resources.

INFORMATION ARCHITECTURE

Information architecture (IA) is about finding logical ways to organize your website content so that your users can make educated guesses about where to find what they are looking for. If users cannot easily figure out how your site is organized, they will become frustrated and leave. If you are familiar with using websites, you are already putting this concept into practice every time you click around a new website looking for content. For example, if you visit retail websites, the website

33

sections are usually grouped together via department. A library website may also be similarly arranged by department. However, always think about your users when organizing your website—do they expect to see all event listings together, or do they expect to find events sorted by age group?

WordPress offers four main ways to organize your content: by menu, category, tag, or page hierarchy. You will learn more about these features in the next section.

IA Tips

- Use the simplest term that is understood by your users (e.g., *book* instead of *monograph* for a public library).
- Try to reduce the number of clicks a user has to make to find your content from your website's home page.
- Three clicks are usually the ideal amount of clicks from your home page to the content.
- Your navigation should remain consistent throughout your website.
- Use "breadcrumbs." These are usually located on the lower left under the site's logo. They show how "deep" you are in a site. For example, *Home > Events > Kids* means you are looking at events for kids. Each breadcrumb link (except the final one on the right) should be a link to back to that section.
- Is your content easy to read? While a lot of IA is involved with navigation, your content needs to be accessible and easy to understand for your target audience.
- Check for broken links.[6]
- Remove unnecessary words and phrases. People have short attention spans when reading online, so keep it snappy!

SECURITY

Anything you put on the Web is vulnerable to attacks from hackers. An attack can overwhelm your web server so that your website shuts down—which is referred to as a denial-of-service (DOS) attack. The online group Anonymous uses this method to punish their targets. Another attack may break into your website and post malicious content or change the log-in information in an effort to lock you out of your site. So, while many hackers may be intent on causing your site personal chaos, others are more dangerous.

If your website allows users to create accounts, you are now dealing with people's personal information. This information can range from simply an e-mail address to a user's credit card or Social Security numbers. Each year, many big-name websites have their security efforts thwarted by hackers who then have access to their users' data. Whenever this happens, the security broach usually makes the news. This creates a public-relations nightmare for the organization as they try to fix the damage not only to their website but also to their reputation.

Simple Ways to Beef Up WordPress Security

Fortunately, the WordPress community puts in a lot of effort to secure the software. You can protect your website from many attacks simply by keeping your website's core software, theme, and plugins up to date. Next, when you create your first account, skip the rookie mistake of naming your administrator account "admin." This common username will help ease the path for intruders to break into your website. Keep your passwords strong. While current wisdom holds that a secure password is a combination of uppercase and lowercase letters, a symbol, and a number, Randall Munroe—the smart guy behind the XKCD web comic—explains the problem with this approach. As argued in the "Password Strength" comic, the current password guidelines means you are creating passwords that are easy for computers to guess. You are better off using random words with no numbers or symbols.[7] Of course, take this with a grain of salt and do your own research. Many websites will not allow you to create a password without using a bizarre combination of symbols, uppercase, and numbers anyway.

Advanced WordPress Security

Now that your site has been set up with the basics of security, you can work on more advanced tasks. For example, you can often discover if a website is run on WordPress by simply adding /wp-admin to the end of the home page's URL. I used this method a lot when scouting websites for this book. You should protect this page from casual users attempting to log in here. Next, lock down your website's directories. A detailed listing of how to do these advanced options and more is located on the WordPress Codex.[8]

Check appendix B for more resources.

ACCESSIBILITY

At this point in the process of thinking about your website, you have identified your primary and secondary audiences. Have you thought about users with disabilities? Disabilities include auditory, cognitive, neurological, physical, speech, and visual impairments.[9] A disability that makes it hard to use a computer may be permanent, or it may be temporary, such as a broken wrist. People's bodies also often become weaker as they grow older.

The United States has two laws dealing with accessibility: the Americans with Disabilities Act (ADA) and the Rehabilitation Act Amendments, also known as Section 508.[10] These two laws outline specific requirements on how to make websites accessible to people with disabilities. While the laws are specifically geared at federal government agencies, your library should work to meet the guidelines set in these two laws. Additionally the World Wide Web Consortium (W3C), which oversees the Web, has also published guidelines, called the Web Accessibility Initiative.[11] Library websites still fall short of meeting Section 508 standards.[12] By planning ahead, accessibility is only 10 percent of your web development time. However, if you forego accessibility in your planning, "your organization can expect double the cost and effort to fix accessibility issues after the fact."[13]

To meet the bare basics of accessibility for your website:

- Make sure the contrast between text and the background is high.
- Include descriptions of your images through alternative (alt) text code, which shows up for screen readers and when the image is hovered over.
- Be mindful of colorblindness; for example, do not put red text on a green background, and vice versa.
- Closed captioning and transcripts should accompany video and audio whenever possible.
- Menus made up of images should have alt text.
- It should be possible to navigate your site by a keyboard alone.
- Your text should be resizable.
- Turn off the images on your website to see if your content still makes sense.
- View your website in gray scale to check if your use of color has a meaningful impact on the understanding and usability of your website.

MOBILE WEBSITES

It is no longer a question of whether your website should be mobile friendly, but whether you should have a mobile website, an app, or both. In April 2012, Pew Internet found that 88 percent of American adults have a cellphone, 55 percent of adult cellphone owners use their phone to go online, and 31 percent of those users report that their phone is how they mostly go online.[14] The percentage of your website users who are accessing your site through their mobile device depends a lot on your patron population's unique characteristics. Factors that may affect whether your users access your site from a mobile device include their economics, their cell network capabilities, their ability to operate Internet-capable phones, and their awareness of whether you even have a website. The number of mobile web users will continue to grow each year as smartphone penetration increases. Mobile access is not limited to cellphones but also includes tablets and laptop access.

Mobile Website

A traditional mobile website is a site that has been specifically built for mobile devices. You may notice this on a smartphone if the URL includes the word *mobile* in the address. This may be a completely separate website than your main website; these mobile-specific sites may be a stripped down version of the main website with fewer features.

The latest trend for mobile is to build a responsive website that accordingly adjusts its appearance depending on the width of the browser. Web designer Ethan Marcotte introduced the concept of responsive web design in May 2010.[15] Using Marcotte's techniques, you build one website and it will work on desktops, tablets, and mobile phones. Further resources about responsive web design are included in appendix B.

Mobile App

The other option is to have an app that is downloaded to a user's phone. Once the app is installed, the user clicks on it to get started. Then the app either acts as a URL shortcut and opens their mobile web browser, or it takes them to a fully functional and self-contained app. Common features of library apps include the catalog, hours, directions, and telephone number. For other examples of what patrons are looking for in library mobile apps, see the Digital Shift's 2012 article on this topic.[16]

WordPress and Mobile

The WordPress community has responded to the challenges of needing mobile websites by going in all three directions. There are responsive themes and plugins to strip your site down to a mobile version (using a mobile plugin may make your site look like all other sites that use this plugin, so you should customize your site's appearance). As for updating your website on the go, you can download a WordPress app that is available for a variety of mobile platforms.[17] For WordPress.org users, there are currently apps on the Android and iOS app markets.

ANALYTICS

Back in the 1990s and early 2000s, it was popular for webmasters to proudly display a site visitor counter on their website. Nowadays websites are usually more discrete with their statistics. It is important to track how visitors interact with your site, for it tells you how the site is used after launch, which sections are the most relevant, how well your marketing campaigns are doing, and so on. You can then use the numbers gathered through analytics to show to your stakeholders for further decision making.

When viewing your analytics, you will come across a number of confusing terms. While you can gain a lot of insight from just looking at the data presented, it is helpful to have an understanding of what the terms refer to. Pay special attention to the difference between the terms *bounce rate* and *exit rate*.

Key Terms

Bounce rate. The number of times users visit your site and then leave or "bounces" away from that initial page instead of going to another page on your website.

Browser. Check to see if people are using modern browsers or if you need to really support ancient browsers.

Exit rate. The number of times a particular page serves as the final page your users look at after they have viewed several pages on your website.

Length of visit. The total amount of time a visitor is on your website.

Operating system. Which operating systems are used by your patrons, which helps you know how to best design your website. Look for mobile results as well since those operating systems may not be the same as the desktop users.

Referral. A web domain that directs people to your website; for example, Google.com or Facebook.com.

Google Analytics

A popular and free way to analyze your website is through Google Analytics.[18] Sign-up is simple; afterward, you cut and paste the Javascript code from Google into your website. Or you can use a plugin to add Google Analytics.[19] Google Analytics is the most popular analytics software for the libraries in this book.

Some features you can track:

- How many people visit your site (new users versus returning users)
- How long people are staying on your website
- What browsers people are using
- Which pages are the most popular

Bitly.com

If you are using social media for your library or project, you will no doubt be posting links. Since most URLs are long and unwieldy to share, you should look into using a URL shortening service. Bitly.com takes your long URL and changes it into a short link that is much friendlier on sites such as Twitter.[20] Using your shortened link, you can then tap in and track how many times that link is being clicked. Recent features on Bitly include being able to add notes to remind yourself where and why you posted a particular link.

Some features:

- If you add a plus sign to the end of any link (e.g., http://bit.ly/abcdef+), you can check others' link stats.

39

- You can write a custom short link, so if the keyword is available, you can have something more memorable at the tail of the URL than a random set of letters.

FUTURE PLANNING

Let's be honest: no one knows the future. However, you can establish plans to help your site continue to grow and develop. Your primary priority is to make sure that your website can be updated and maintained even after you have left the web developer position. I would recommend documenting your procedures online somewhere. For my web projects, I use Google Docs (now called Google Drive). I share the document with my supervisor and anyone else who will be working to develop the website. Most content contributors will not need to see all the gritty details about how the site is put together.

Create a Style Guide

You need to establish style guidelines to maintain a consistent appearance across your website. That is, what text should be bolded, where images are placed, how URLs are constructed, and so on. The more information and visual examples you include, the easier it will be to ensure and enforce that your website continues to be uniform. Ideally, you would create your style guide sometime between planning your website and building it.[21]

Prepare a Successor

You will want to set up a system for training future website maintainers. There should always be someone in your library who knows how to manage and update the website. In the short term, this person will take over while you are on vacation or at a conference. In the long term, this person could step in and run the website on their own if you had a sudden departure. You want to avoid a situation where your library's website is inaccessible to staff.

Establish Clear Content Guidelines

You want to make sure that your website can handle adding new content. Content creep is when information outside of your original established categories starts appearing onto your website. For example, your site originally had sections for adults, teens, and children. Suddenly, a department decides that you need to add a preteen section. While this age group may indeed be caught between toddlers and teenagers, you can run into a nightmare when everyone wants to break up your website categories even further. You can nip this in the bud by making sure to establish clear guidelines regarding the purpose of each section of your website and standing by those decisions. If you do not have a clear plan on how new information is placed on the site, you risk your site drifting into incoherence.

NOTES

1. Shannon Hyman, "Creating Virtual Spaces," *Knowledge Quest* 41, no. 5 (May 2013): 36–39, *Academic Search Premier*, EBSCO *host,* accessed July 26, 2013.
2. Google Drive, http://drive.google.com; Trello, www.trello.com.
3. Wikipedia, "Multi-touch," http://en.wikipedia.org/wiki/Multi-touch.
4. Internet World Stats, "Internet Users in North America: June 30, 2012," www.internetworldstats.com/stats14.htm.
5. For the current requirements, please see http://wordpress.org/about/requirements/.
6. There is a plugin for that: Broken Link Checker, http://wordpress.org/extend/plugins/broken-link-checker/.
7. Randall Munroe, "Password Strength," http://xkcd.com/936/.
8. WordPress.org, "Hardening WordPress," http://codex.wordpress.org/Hardening_WordPress.
9. World Wide Web Consortium, "Diversity of Abilities," 2012, www.w3.org/WAI/intro/people-use-web/diversity#diversity.
10. US Department of Justice, "Accessibility of State and Local Government Websites to People with Disabilities," 2003, www.ada.gov/websites2.htm.
11. Web Accessibility Initiative, www.w3.org/WAI/.
12. Jim Blansett, "Digital Discrimination: Ten Years after Section 508, Libraries Still Fall Short of Addressing Disabilities Online," August 15, 2008, http://lj.libraryjournal.com/2008/08/ljarchives/digital-discrimination/.
13. Catharine McNally, "Integrating Accessibility into your Public Sector Site," *Acquia* video, 60:00, June 7, 2012, www.acquia.com/resources/acquia-tv/conference/integrating-accessibility-your-public-sector-site-june-7-2012.
14. Joanna Brenner, "Pew Internet: Mobile," 2012, www.pewinternet.org/Commentary/2012/February/Pew-Internet-Mobile.aspx.
15. Ethan Marcotte, "Responsive Web Design," 2010, www.alistapart.com/articles/responsive-web-design.

16. Lisa Carlucci Thomas, "The State of Mobile in Libraries 2012," 2012, www
.thedigitalshift.com/2012/02/mobile/the-state-of-mobile-in-libraries-2012/.

17. WordPress.com, "Apps for WordPress.com," http://en.support.wordpress.com/apps/.

18. Google Analytics, www.google.com/analytics/.

19. Joost de Valk, "Google Analytics for WordPress," http://wordpress.org/extend/plugins/
google-analytics-for-wordpress/.

20. Bitly, https://bitly.com/.

21. Check out MailChimp's delightful example of how much fun a style guide can be:
http://voiceandtone.com/.

Chapter Five

Using WordPress

Because installing WordPress is an easy process, it follows that even beginners can build a website in a short amount of time. While WordPress is documented through its own manual called the WordPress Codex, it is not always the most user-friendly.[1] So there are help forums and thousands of users who document their WordPress tips on their own websites. A simple search engine search will bring back posts on any aspect of the platform. Also do not underestimate the WordPress community that exists on every social network. If you are a WordPress.com user, you can also consult the official documentation online.[2]

The content here in part 2 introduces many aspects of the software, with links and additional resources in the appendix. In this chapter, we will look at the content creation tools built into WordPress.

THE DASHBOARD

When you log in to your WordPress website, the screen you are presented with is the dashboard. Here you will be able to manage the entirety of your website from uploading new themes to adding new users. This level of control through the web interface is not always present in other content management systems. WordPress places all the website's controls on the top menu bar and on the left sidebar.

The dashboard described here is for the administrator of the website. Users who have access to post on your website will see modified versions of the dashboard with the appropriate limited options. An introduction to customizing the dashboard can be found in the "Users" section.

Top Menu Bar

As of this writing, the top menu bar is used for quick shortcuts for the most frequent tasks. These include drop-down menus (when you click or hover on a link, the menu of links that appears underneath) to create different types of content and to go back to either the public-facing website or the dashboard. If you have a theme or a plugin that is ready to be updated, you will see a small notification icon in this menu bar. The beauty of the top toolbar is that if you are viewing the edit screen of a post and then want to hop back to the dashboard, you simply click on the dashboard button in the top menu.

Underneath the top menu bar you will occasionally receive a nag screen notification for when the core WordPress software is ready to be updated.

Left Sidebar

All the controls of your website are present in the collapsible left sidebar. Either you can click on a link to go to a page listing all the options under that section, or you can hover your mouse so that a drop-down menu will show you all the options. A sample section is the "General" section. When you hover or click, you are then presented with the choice to adjust a number of settings that affect how WordPress works.

Main Content Screen

When you first install or upgrade WordPress to the latest version, you will see a brief announcement about the latest features or bug fixes. Once you dismiss that message, you then see your overview administrator screen. You can see how many posts and pages are on your website. You can also keep an eye on the total number of comments or how many times suspected spam has been posted. There are also boxes for the latest WordPress news that you can collapse to ignore.

CONTENT CREATION

The point of any website is to share content. This content may be text, audio, visual, or interactive (e.g., a game) in nature. WordPress comes with two different main frameworks for managing content: posts and pages. Each of these content types can contain text, audio, or video. Posts and pages also come with two default fields to enter text: the title and body fields. The term *title* is self-explanatory, while the body is where you put in all your content.

WordPress handles each content type differently for site organization and in real simple syndication (RSS). In the following sections we will learn how posts and pages differ and how to create your own content types.

Page

A page is the content type where you add static content on your website. (*Static* means content that is not updated frequently. Think of your library's "Policies" or "About" page. You type up your library's hours, and that content is not changed until needed.) Of course, you can build an entire website of pages because WordPress does not limit how many pages your site may contain. Using only pages on your website will make your site function more like a traditional website.

Menu Items

So you have your content on your page, but how will you let people know where your page is on your website? Pages can be assigned as main menu items (e.g., an "About" page), while single blog posts cannot traditionally be menu items.

Parent and Child Pages

Pages are organized into hierarchies. Top-level pages are called parent pages which are often then linked to in your main menus. You can have multiple parent pages on your website. Other pages can be assigned to go underneath a parent page. These pages are called the children of the top-level parent page. An example of a parent and child pages would be:

- About Us
  - o Mission Statement
  - o Directions
  - o Hours

In this example, your parent page is called "About Us." Since these are static content pages, your "About Us" page may have a welcome message and a photo of your library. Then each child page—"Mission Statement," "Directions," "Hours"—would be organized underneath the "About Us" page. Parent and child pages are how you organize your site's pages.

Page Order

By default, you can also control which order child pages are listed in. Your order may be alphabetical or any other scheme that makes sense. WordPress gives you the option to assign a page number. The lower the number assigned to a page, the higher in the site's hierarchy the page will be. You can see this more clearly by thinking of the above example with the "About Us" pages. "Mission Statement" is the first page listed under "About Us," since it was the first page created and assigned as a child to "About Us." However, if you decide that "Hours" should be first, you would simply edit the "Hours" page and enter the number 1 in its Order box. You will then need to edit the other pages under "About Us" to make sure they display in the right order.

As you may guess, this manual reordering of pages can get overwhelming fast. Fortunately, there are a number of ways to make this process easier. By installing an add-on for reordering pages, you can then manipulate page hierarchies with ease. These add-ons are called plugins, which we will be covering shortly.

Pages and RSS Feeds

Pages are not displayed in chronological order on your website like posts. In fact, if a user has subscribed to your website's latest updates through a RSS feeder such as Feedly, your new pages will never show up in her RSS feed.[3] WordPress creates RSS feeds only from posts.

Post

Posts are the content type that makes up blogs. On a default WordPress installation, all posts will show up on the front page of your website. The posts are in chronological order so that the newest post is on top. Posts can be made up of text, audio, image, or video content. While pages have static content that is useful and does not change often, posts are often time sensitive. The post content type is ideal for listing upcoming events or keeping a journal on an ongoing project. Traditionally, post links do not go into menus on a website.

Categories

While pages are organized into parent and child pages, posts are organized into categories. On a superficial level, categories are very similar to child pages. When a post is marked as belonging to a particular category, the post will show up underneath that category. However, accessing a particular category is not quite as simple as designating a page as a menu item. Categories are accessed by clicking or hovering on the Posts menu item in the left sidebar.

First, you need to add categories to your website. You create a subcategory by assigning the new category to a parent category. For example, you set up an Events category. Then you add subcategories for Children, Teens, and Adults. Every time an events post is written, it will need to be assigned a subcategory. The best practice seems to be that you would mark both the parent category as well as the subcategory.

To view the list of all posts assigned to a category, you would go back to the Category menu item in Posts. By clicking on the number of posts on the far right of each category, you can then see a list of all posts in that category. Depending on your site's theme (appearance), your site visitors may be able to see which categories a post has been assigned to. By clicking on the category link, the user is taken to a list of all posts in that category.

Tags

While categories are an attempt at a high-level careful taxonomy system for your site, tags are free ranging. Your post should be carefully categorized; you can add as many tags as you want to add an extra layer of discovery. For instance, if your post is about Amelia Earhart, you may assign her name to a Person category. However, the tags for the post may be *Amelia Earhart, female aviators, missing people*, and so on. Similar to categories, if your theme supports it, you may see a list of post tags displayed whereby clicking on them takes you to a list of all posts that share this tag.

Posts and RSS Feeds

Unlike pages, posts are a natural fit for RSS feeds. When a patron subscribes to updates from your website, all your posts will show up in their RSS feeder. This function is ideal because posts are usually time sensitive. For your site follower, they will receive the update about the latest news from your library shortly after you publish the post.

Reordering Posts

While posts default to chronological order, you can break this flow by marking a post as sticky. A post with this designation will then show up at the top of the list of posts on your websites and "stick" there until you remove it, or until a newer post is also marked as sticky which then displays above the older sticky post. As with pages, there are plugins that you can install to reorder posts. The PostMash Custom plugin works well, but it can be a resource hog.[4] So after you reorder your pages, disable the plugin again.

Page of Posts

To make things more confusing, you can also have a page of posts. However, do not feel too overwhelmed—WordPress's default blog setup is simply a page of all your posts published on the website. To create your own page of posts, you will need to create categories. This way your page of posts knows which posts it will display. For example, say you have menu items for your adult, teen, and children's events. Each event will have its own category with a name that corresponds to the correct age group (e.g., Teen). You would then create a page of posts that would display only events categorized as teen events. The page of posts method also works with tags.

Methods

There are several different ways to create a page of posts. The easiest way is to create a custom menu. First, you will need to find the URL for the category so you can set it as a menu link. You can find the URL for a category by creating a post with that category, then viewing the published post. Hover your mouse over your category link. In our example, this would be teens. By right-clicking and copying that URL, you can set it as a menu item in your primary navigation (which we look at in the "Navigation" section below). Keep in mind that not all themes will show a list of categories and tags for each post. Not all WordPress.com themes have the option to create a custom menu, but instructions can be found in their support pages.[5]

The second way to create a page of posts is to use a plugin like Pages Posts.[6] Because you should limit the number of plugins you are using on your website, I would recommend using the first method—doing it manually—instead of relying on a plugin.

The third method is the most complex but will give you the greatest customization. By default, WordPress creates pages of posts via categories and tags. However, you may not appreciate the URL (which usually looks like /category/teens or /tag/teens) or even how the page is laid out. In order to change this layout on self-hosted installations, you will need to make a new page of posts template. The WordPress Codex has a sample template that can get you started.[7] This method is time consuming and advanced, but it allows you to make your page of posts look just the way you want.

Custom Content

Custom Posts

If you've been looking at WordPress while reading this section, you may have noticed that pages and posts have a lot of unnecessary boxes cluttering the screen. On a post screen, for example, aside from having the title and body box, you also have tag, category, and featured image boxes. Plugins can also add even more boxes. So if your website does not use categories, having a category box would be very confusing to your writers. Or you may want to use WordPress to build a simple catalog. You would need to have fields such as *Author*, *ISBN*, *Title*, *Publication Date*, and *Summary* that would need to be filled out for each book. You could try to use a regular post or page for this and have a check list for content creators to try and ensure that each book entry's fields are completely filled out. However, you would probably notice inconsistent metadata appearing on your site almost immediately whenever someone forgets to fill a field. To fix this issue, you would create a custom post type that is available only for self-hosted WordPress installations.

The process to create a custom post type is not overly complicated. While the information on the WordPress Codex is comprehensive, it is a bit difficult to make the leap from reading their instructions to creating your own custom post type.[8] Fortunately, the online community has come together and created several detailed tutorials that provide you with code and images on how to make your own post type. There are also plugins which can ease the process.

More Information

- The Complete Guide to Custom Post Types
  http://wp.smashingmagazine.com/2012/11/08/complete-guide-custom
  -post-types/
- Create Your First WordPress Custom Post Type
  http://blog.teamtreehouse.com/create-your-first-wordpress-custom-post
  -type
- A Guide to WordPress Custom Post Types: Creation, Display and Meta Boxes
  http://wp.tutsplus.com/tutorials/plugins/a-guide-to-wordpress-custom
  -post-types-creation-display-and-meta-boxes/
- Custom Post Type UI
  http://wordpress.org/extend/plugins/custom-post-type-ui/
- Types
  http://wordpress.org/extend/plugins/types/

49

Other examples of custom post types include but are not limited to: databases, event listings, staff profiles, and program information.

Custom Fields

If you need to add additional fields to your content types, you have the option of adding custom fields.[9] An example custom field for a student's weather tracking blog would be a daily weather field. This field may have a select list of options such as sunny, cloudy, or snowing. The purpose of creating a custom field for this purpose would be so that you would always remember to select the option to display today's weather at your library. In a library setting, you may want a custom field for citations. However, creating all these custom fields can be tedious. Instead you may want to just create a new custom post type.

Custom Taxonomies

While you can use the default tags, categories, and parent-child relationships to organize content on your website, it can quickly become overwhelming for content creators. What are all the categories that I need to check off for my database post? Did I miss something? An important job of web developers is to remove such uncertainties from the content producer's mind. WordPress gives you the ability to create custom taxonomies that may only appear on certain custom post types.[10] For example, you may have a custom post type to list staff members on your website. You want a custom taxonomy that gives you the option to check off which department a particular person works for. Your custom taxonomy would appear only on the staff member post type and not on a database or event listing post type.[11]

Feeling confused? Check out the detailed breakdown comparing custom fields to custom post types to custom taxonomies in a post by Joe Foley.[12]

CONCLUSION

In the WordPress eCourses I cotaught with Polly-Alida Farrington, students were routinely tripped up trying to understand when to use a post versus a page. The suggested rules outlined above are embraced across different CMS platforms. Your website can be made up of only posts, or only pages, or a mix of posts and pages. The pages-only option gives a more traditional website experience without any hint of your site looking like a blog.

NOTES

1. WordPress.org, "Codex," http://codex.wordpress.org/.

2. WordPress.com, "Support," http://en.support.wordpress.com/.

3. Feedly, http://feedly.com.

4. opperud.com, "PostMash Custom – custom post order," http://wordpress.org/extend/plugins/postmash-custom/.

5. WordPress.com, "Custom Menus," http://en.support.wordpress.com/menus/.

6. rgubby, "Pages Posts," http://wordpress.org/extend/plugins/pages-posts/.

7. WordPress.org, "A Page of Posts," http://codex.wordpress.org/Pages#A_Page_of_Posts.

8. WordPress.org, "Custom Types," http://codex.wordpress.org/Post_Types#Custom_Types.

9. WordPress.org, "Custom Fields," http://codex.wordpress.org/Custom_Fields.

10. WordPress.org, "Taxonomies," http://codex.wordpress.org/Taxonomies.

11. *Smashing Magazine* gives a great overview of how to use and create custom taxonomies. See Kevin Leary, "How to Create Custom Taxonomies in WordPress," January 4, 2012, http://wp.smashingmagazine.com/2012/01/04/create-custom-taxonomies-wordpress/.

12. Joe Foley, "WordPress Custom Fields vs. Custom Post Types vs. Custom Taxonomies," March 7, 2012, http://wpmu.org/wordpress-custom-fields-vs-custom-posts-types-vs-custom-taxonomies/.

51

Chapter Six

Themes

I f you have ever used a hosted blog service such as LiveJournal, Tumblr, or Twit-ter, you are familiar with the concept of being able to go into the settings and pick a new theme to change the appearance of your personal blog. The parts of your blog that can be changed are the color, the background image, the font, or even the arrangement of different sections of the page. For most blog services like this, a simple click of the button is all it takes to get a whole new feel to your website.

WordPress works in a similar way. If you have a WordPress.com account, you can select one of the available themes, and with a few clicks, change your site's appearance. Themes are found on your dashboard by clicking on the Appearance tab. If you pay for the annual custom CSS upgrade, you can alter the colors and fonts on your website.[1] On a self-hosted version of WordPress, you can install any of the thousands of themes which are available through the official repository.[2] Since this version of WordPress is completely your own, you have complete freedom to control the appearance of your website. In the next section of the book, we will look more in depth at web design principles, which can help you pick the best theme for your project.

A warning: you should download free themes only from the official WordPress .org repository because they have been verified as safe to use.

WHAT MAKES A THEME

Each WordPress theme is made up of individual files that all end with the extension *php*. These files are known as templates. A single template file includes code instructions that tell the browser how to display the website. Many themes include a header.php, a footer.php, and templates for sidebars, single pages, single posts, the home page, and so much more. Also included are CSS style sheets and perhaps Javascript files. Together all these files turn WordPress into a content management system. By separating each area of the website into its own section, you can edit one file to change the way that section looks on every page on the website. For example, you can add a search box to the header.php and no matter where you go on the website, there will be a search box in the header. If you were building a non-CMS website, you would need to copy that header text on every single HTML document that makes up your website. Any time you made a change, you would have to go back through your entire website to change each page.

54

WHAT TO LOOK FOR IN A THEME

A popular question in my WordPress classes is about suggestions for WordPress themes special to a library website. If you are building a special-project website, you may need to look for something more specific. It is difficult to recommend one theme suitable for libraries. In general, if you do not have time to devote to your website, setting up and maintaining a complex theme may be out of your league. When reviewing a theme, check the ratings and preview it (if you are browsing themes through your dashboard) to see how much effort you will need to put in to make the theme work for you. A popular choice is magazine themes, also referred to as newspaper themes. These themes are the most specific and complex themes meant to display large amounts of information in a cohesive fashion. You will see themes like this on many newspaper websites.

When you choose a theme, keep in mind that you will probably need to customize your WordPress site in some way to make the best use of the theme. These changes may be as simple as rearranging items around your sidebar (e.g., your site's secondary links or Flickr photostream) or setting up new content types to take advantage of a particular theme's built-in image slideshow. Then someday when you are ready to revamp your website's appearance again with a new theme, you will spend a lot of time pushing your site's content around to fit the new theme. This is a time-consuming process, so you will probably not change your theme too often.

OBTAINING THEMES

There are four different ways to obtain a new theme for your website. First, you can find a free theme using the methods listed below on how to browse for a theme. Or you can pay for a premade theme, which is referred to as a premium theme. These themes often have special functions or advanced customization options that do not come with free themes. A few well-known premium theme developers are WooThemes or ThemeForest.[3] If you want a unique theme, you can hire a freelancer to design one for you. Or you can design a new theme in-house utilizing your own library's web talent. Your unique theme may be entirely new or could be based upon another theme.

HOW TO FIND OFFICIAL THEMES

WordPress.com

Go to the theme section of WordPress (http://theme.wordpress.com/). You can browse themes by trending (i.e., recent popularity), alphabetical order, general popularity, or when they were created, or by premium themes you can purchase. If you are browsing for themes through your dashboard, you can also see sponsored themes. If you want to narrow down the two hundred–plus official themes, you can use the Find a Theme button. Themes can then be searched for by keyword or filtered by features. The more features a theme has coming out of the box, the less altering the theme needs to make it your site's theme. Filter categories are color, number of columns, how wide the site is in your browser, special features, subject (e.g., business, education), or style (e.g., clean). You can also find themes by logging into your dashboard, then clicking on Appearance, then Themes.

WordPress.org

Go to the theme repository (http://wordpress.org/extend/themes/). You will notice that the self-hosted version of WordPress's themes directory is much less user friendly than the hosted version. Themes here are submitted by the WordPress community by users with various levels of technical skill. Since this version of WordPress gives you full-control, you can download any theme here and truly make it your own. You can search by keyword or by tag—or if you love to filter, you can narrow your results by color, column, width, feature, and subject. The filtering option allows for checking multiple items off per category so you can find that perfect theme.

HOW TO PREVIEW AND INSTALL THEMES

WordPress.com

Depending on how you are finding themes, you can either see a generic demonstration of the theme in action or see how a particular theme looks using your current content. If you are browsing through the main themes site, click on Live Demo to see a generic version of the theme. However, if you are searching from within your dashboard interface, click on Live Preview to see how your site would look wearing this theme. The preview may need some adjustments, as the new theme may have different features from your current site, such as a large image area. Once you find a theme you like, you can click on Activate to use it on your site.

WordPress.org

There are three ways to add a new theme to your website. First, you can download a theme directly to your computer and then upload the theme through your WordPress dashboard interface. Or you can browse for themes from within your dashboard as described above; then just click to download and activate the chosen theme. Finally, you can upload a theme via the themes directory on your server. Once your theme is installed, you can activate it by going to the dashboard and clicking on Appearance; you will then see all the themes available for your website. Simply click Activate underneath the theme that you would like to use on your site. As with the WordPress.com website, you can preview all themes that you find through your dashboard before activating them on your live website.

CUSTOMIZE THEMES

How to Customize Your Theme

The ability to customize your website depends on how your site is being hosted. For a WordPress.com user, as noted earlier, for a price you can edit only your style .css page to make changes to your website's appearance. While these changes can give your site a drastic makeover, it is not as customizable as a hosted site. Multisite users face similar restrictions to hosted WordPress.com websites; they can activate only themes that were already made available by the multisite administrator.

If you are hosting your own WordPress installation, you have complete freedom to customize your theme. Themes can be edited by going to the Appearance menu then clicking on Editor. Each template and style sheet that makes up the website can then be accessed for editing in the browser. However, this can be time consuming and dangerous as a browser crash can eliminate your work. It is therefore better to use FTP to download the theme files to your server and work on them on your desktop. You can then auto-save your files back to the server or copy your changes back onto the server. Either way, make sure to have backups before you start theme work each day. However, you can also work smarter and use a child theme or a theme framework.

Child Themes

If you are working in the code to customize your site's theme, you should think about using a child theme. A child theme allows you to install one theme (referred to here as the parent) that has the functions and somewhat close to the appearance that you want for your website. Then you create a second theme (the child theme) that holds all the customizations that you want to make to the parent theme. The point is that the parent theme gives you a strong foundation that you want to use while the child theme lets you customize things further by overriding some features. For example, say your parent theme almost matches your ideal website vision. It's just that the background color and the header text are the wrong colors. You could dive into this theme's code to make the adjustments. However, when a new update for that theme is released and you install it, all of your changes will be overwritten. While this may not be a big deal if you changed only a couple items, it can cause chaos if you customized the theme extensively.

Creating a child theme is very easy. You will need to access the server that WordPress is installed upon to create the only required file: a new style.css file. This new style.css will override the parent theme's style.css file. Therefore you should make sure to copy the content of the parent's style.css into your child theme's style .css in order to keep the aspects of the original's theme that you liked. If you do not, you will get a completely unstyled website. Also, any file you place in the child theme's directory that matches a file name in the parent directory will supersede the parent theme's file of the same name. If you do not have access to your website's server, you can also use the One-Click Child Theme plugin to help you set up a child theme.[4] However, the better method is to create the child theme on the server.

Read the child theme section on WordPress Codex for specific and current information.[5]

Theme Framework

Another option is to use a theme framework for your website. A theme framework is not meant to be used as the actual theme on your website but facilitates developing your own theme. There are two varieties of theme frameworks: a code library that is "included in the Theme's functions.php file" or a very basic starter theme that gives the web designer a platform to create child themes from.[6] A theme framework often incorporates extensive customizations that make it easier to design and develop your own theme.

Theme frameworks may be free or can be purchased. A couple of free theme frameworks are Bones and Toolbox.[7] Some premium theme frameworks include Headway, Thesis, and Genesis; Genesis is used by the Lanier Theological Library, as discussed in chapter 15.[8]

WEB DESIGN

There are thousands of themes available for WordPress. The criteria for judging whether a theme is appropriate for your needs are very subjective. However, you can begin to make some decisions on which themes to investigate if you have a basic understanding of web design principles. This section offers only the briefest of introductions to each topic, but it should be enough to get you started.

The important thing to remember here is that once you start to learn about web design and start to develop designs yourself, it is easy to get overwhelmed. Know from the start that there will always be a design that is better than your own and that what is appealing to one person may not be so to another. Many of the professional web designers who write books and freelance for well-known companies are highly dedicated professionals. They can often afford to focus on learning everything about one aspect of web design, development, or programming. As a person who works at a library, your job is to make something that works. It is vital that your website not be unattractive, but you can always work on improving your skills and the design as you have time.

Additional resources for these web design topics can be found in appendix B.

Page Sections

Throughout this book, I reference the different sections of a website. Understanding what these sections are called and what they contain will help you in your discussions with web designers and in your research. The sections below are listed in their traditional flow from the top to the bottom of a web page.

Header

The header is the very top of any web page, and usually prominent on the home page of any website. The content in this section usually includes the site's logo (on the left), the site's name, and the top-level navigation. Other popular items are a tag line (e.g., "Your trusted news resource"), a log-in button or form, and a search box.

Navigation

The navigation may be part of the header, or it may appear in a sidebar. For many WordPress websites, the navigation is considered to be part of the header in the site's organization.

Breadcrumbs

Have you ever felt lost on a website? If you check the top left (on left-to-right websites) of a website underneath the site's logo, you will probably see a set of links that usually start with the word *Home*. Each link that progresses to the right of *Home* is a step deeper into the website's hierarchy. If you get lost, you can usually click on a breadcrumb to go up a level.

Body

The body section is also the main content area for your web page. Here is where your page or post content is displayed. Your text and media will appear here. This section is usually the largest and most eye-catching part of your site because it is where most of your visitor's time will be spent looking at the content that is displayed here.

Sidebar

Sidebars are, true to their name, located to the side of the main content on the page. Your website's theme may have multiple sidebars or none at all. Navigational elements are usually in a left sidebar while advertisements are traditionally placed in the right sidebar. Be aware that many online users are used to the convention of ads on the right and therefore may be "blind" to anything on the far right side of a page.

Footer

The footer is at the opposite end of the page from the header, at the very bottom. Footers are often neglected by site designers, but do not fall for that trap! You can add additional menus here, contact information, your latest tweet, a photo stream, and more.

Web Technologies

Websites are made using web languages. There are many languages out there for both web designers and web developers to use in building websites. You can get away with knowing no web languages while using WordPress, but to truly customize your site without paying a separate designer, you may want to try picking up a little bit on the below four most common languages. Suggested resources can be found in appendix B.

HTML

At the very bottom of everything, hypertext markup language (HTML) is what really created the Web that we know today. With HTML's creation, web pages were able to be linked to one another, and that interconnectivity created what is sometimes called the World Wide Web. For your purposes, HTML is the tiny bits of code that makes text into a paragraph, a link, boldface type, an item on a list, embedded content such as a video, and so much more. If you are using the Visual Editor in WordPress as you type, you can mark up your text to add links and bold text. Then, if you switch over to the HTML tab (which is next to the Visual Editor to the top left of your body box), you can see the HTML that is the source of your page. HTML allows you to mark up text to be a paragraph, a header, or even body text.

CSS

An important concept of the modern web is that you want to separate your code for your website's content from the code for your overall design. Cascading style sheets (CSS) is the language that allows you to place (usually) all your style information in one location and refer to it everywhere on the website without having to type out the same style code over and over. For instance, let's say that you want every title on your website to be red, very large, bold, and set in New Times Roman. While you could manually add *all* that information *every single time* you add a title element to a web page, by defining all that information with a simple style rule, the only thing you need to do is mark up a title with that style rule's name. CSS also controls the layout of how pages look. For example, if you want your sidebar to always appear on the left side of the website, you would use CSS to put the sidebar on the left. Overall, CSS is the very close twin of HTML, and they should be used together.

Javascript

So if HTML and CSS are twins working together to display content correctly, Javascript is their cousin that adds interactivity to the mix. If you have ever seen a pop-up box on a website or submitted a web form, you have interacted with Javascript. You can build a useful website without a drop of Javascript on it, but it will be a much more engaging experience for your end user if he can interact with your site.

PHP

Hypertext pre-processor (PHP—yep, the acronym is not in the right order) is somewhat like the server-side version of Javascript. WordPress and other CMS platforms use PHP to build their webpages. Remember earlier when discussing how WordPress is made up of files that end with *php*? This is what that suffix was referring to. While in the past, you would create individual HTML files that would include the same header, sidebars, footer, and other content on every single page of your website, PHP allows those sections to be housed separately from the content so they need to be set up only once—and then they will be called in on every single page. You can see this for yourself by going to the Appearances menu and clicking on Editor. You will see that each WordPress theme comes with a whole slew of PHP files that control every section of a page, top to bottom. If you decide that you want to add a tagline to your website, you would go to the header.php file to add it and the tagline would appear on every page. Back in the old way of doing things, you would have to edit every single page of the possibly thousands on your entire website to do the same thing.

61

Fonts and Colors

The appearance of your website is very important. A bank website that looks like it's hanging on from the 1990s will appear less trustworthy than a competitor who has a slick, shiny modern design. User perception is crucial. So while your chosen theme will do most of the heavy work of setting up the appearance of your website, you can make sure to follow a few good design rules. Also be aware that different cultures view different colors as having different significances. For example, in the Western world, brides traditionally wear white. In eastern cultures, white is the color of death. While the meaning of a color may not seem to have a direct relationship to how your library is perceived, it is still something to keep in mind. Below are some font and color tips that will help make your site successful.

Tips

- Pick only a couple of fonts (e.g., Georgia) and stick to them!
- Serif fonts have little feet on the ends (e.g., Times New Roman), while sans serif do not (e.g., Arial). Sans serif is more readable on screen.
- When making decisions about which fonts to use, remember to always include serif or sans-serif at the end of CSS declaration so that if all else fails, your site's font will retain an approximation of your creative vision. (E.g., p {font-family: "Times New Roman", Georgia, serif;})
- Keep your text color in high contrast to the background—for example, do not place red text on a black background.
- If you have a background image, make sure that the text on top of the image is readable.
- Make sure that your font size is large enough. Good accessibility rules say that you should give people buttons to easily resize the font to their needs.
- Try to avoid using colors together that are indistinguible for those who are colorblind, such as red and green.
- There are a limited number of fonts that are considered "web safe" in that every computer usually renders them true. However, you can now use web fonts that can be linked for usability, which gives you more options.[9]

Layout

Aside from noticing any eye-popping colors when you first visit a website, the next thing people will notice is the site's layout. The term *web layout* refers to how content is arranged on the screen. Since web design often still bears hallmarks of print publication, you may see well-arranged and clear columns such as the paper and online versions of *The New Yorker*. Or the website seems to drop layout all together and instead uses a large embedded video to fill the screen. However, even in these cases is the layout on display. You may notice it in the way the video is arranged in the center or to the left or right. The point here is that layout is something you are already familiar with as someone who has used word processing software and read a few things in your life. Website layouts also run in trends. In the early 2000s, all sites were aligned to the left. Then center alignment took over—which has increased as more sites simplify their design to be more tablet friendly.

Balanced Design

The yin-yang symbol is so pleasing because it is in perfect harmony. Your eye swoops around, following the curves and the way the two pieces fit so well together with the black-and-white contrast. Your website should maintain a similarly balanced appearance. It is difficult to describe what is meant in a short amount of space, but visualize it this way. If you have a large item (text, graphic, or video) on the left side of your website, there should be something on the right to balance out the appearance.

Balance is also affected by more than just big blocks of content. Patrick Cox, in his article "Developing Balance in Web Design," describes balance as "the way design elements interact with each other in a composition."[10] He describes the different types of balance arrangements as horizontal, vertical, radial, symmetrical, and asymmetrical. Balance is achieved in practice by using the elements of size, color, shape, value (i.e., contrast), and position. His article is a quick guide to explaining how to recognize the elements of a balanced web design. In all cases, balance is achieved by giving a balanced number of focus points. One object may dominate, but it should not be in a field by itself. Other items on the page will support it by drawing the eye to move around the page.

Grid System

To better understand balance, a web designer should be familiar with the Swiss grid (among other names). The basic principle is that everything should be aligned with one another. If your eyes were scanning a poster, for example, all lines of text should have the same starting edge unless there is a significant reason why a particular line is indented. These alignments apply horizontally as well in most cases. You want all objects on your website to be lined up otherwise it will stick out. Sometimes you *want* something to stick out as a way to draw attention to the item.

63

However, as my graphic design teacher said, you want these nonsequiturs to look intentional. So if you push something out of alignment, make sure to go big with it!

An easy way to make an attractive website is through a careful use of columns. Websites are usually described as being one to *x* number of columns across. Each column does not need to be the same width. A website with a large content area and a thin column next to it is still considered to have a two-column design. While most websites are laid out in columns, note that this may not always be so on more experimental websites.

If you search for *"grid system"* you will come across a multitude and confusing array of web design frameworks that are called grid systems. These frameworks tend to work off a web design layout that is 960 pixels wide (an iPad's width). A grid system framework is great for rapid web design development, as you lay out your site in columns and rows. The best way to get familiar with how grid systems work is to look at an example such as 960 Grid System.[11] If you are just learning how to build websites and use WordPress, grid system frameworks may be out of your league for the time being. As you mature into a sophisticated web designer, you will want to come back to grid systems.

"The Fold"

Because web design still calls upon print design in some of its foundations, there is a concept known as "the fold." Visualize a newspaper sitting in a newspaper box. You can see only the top half of the paper. Everything that is below the center horizontal fold is obscured to you. While the Web does not share all the limitations of print, many people still use the fold concept for websites. It can still be true on many websites that any content that is put below the fold—the area that is not visible unless the visitor scrolls down the screen—will not be viewed. However, others have argued that the fold no longer applies in web design since most Internet users know to scroll down to see more content. What you can take from this discussion is to put your most vital information where a user does not need to scroll to see it. Each website's vital content differs, so think about your library's users, your website statistics, and what you wish to push as an organization to determine what is most important to display.

Static versus Moving Layout Designs

As you navigate around the Web you may notice that a website appears different depending on the browser and screen size of your device. Some websites may sprawl outwards and consume every pixel of your monitor to the point that content is spread far apart (a liquid layout). Other websites are dead set—they are only so wide and stay absolutely fixed in this position (referred to as fixed width). Then there are websites that appear to readjust themselves to be attractive at various browser widths. The website's design seems intentional (unlike the liquid layout, whose content is trying to make sure it covers the exact same amount of screen size even if it looks ridiculously too wide or too small.) Web designs that adjust their content in an intentional way are being responsive or adaptive.

There is no absolute layout design principle that is best among liquid, fixed, and responsive. Each design is an attempt to make websites usable across an ever increasing range of devices that have no universal size. The current fashion is to use responsive web design that works on the principle of planning out how your website will look on a mobile device (usually a phone), then on a tablet, then on a desktop computer. You start with the most basic elements that are required and make sure they appear in an attractive and usable manner on a cellphone. Then you can add to the complexity of the site's design as you design for larger screens. The goal here is that you have one website with a single code base that can be rendered on all devices. In the past, you would build one website for your desktop users and another for your mobile users. Trying to keep these splintered websites in sync was a nightmare. Thus came along responsive web design, which ties together several preexisting principles into one neat package. To use responsive design, you need a flexible grid and flexible media, and to use media queries. Responsive web design is fascinating and can fill hundreds of articles, dozens of books, and more. The best resource to get started is Ethan Marcotte's book *Responsive Web Design*, as discussed in the "Layout" section.

65

NOTES

1. WordPress.com, "Custom CSS," http://en.support.wordpress.com/custom-design/custom-css/.

2. WordPress.org, "Themes Directory," http://wordpress.org/themes/.

3. WooThemes, www.woothemes.com; ThemeForest, http://themeforest.net/.

4. tychay, "One-Click Child Theme," http://wordpress.org/extend/plugins/one-click-child-theme/.

5. WordPress.org, "Child Themes," http://codex.wordpress.org/Child_Themes.

6. WordPress.org, "Theme Frameworks," http://codex.wordpress.org/Theme_Frameworks.

7. Themble, "Bones," http://themble.com/bones/ and Ian Stewart, "Toolbox: An HTML5 WordPress Starter Theme," 2010, http://themeshaper.com/2010/07/02/toolbox-html5-starter-theme/.

8. Headway Themes, "Headway," http://headwaythemes.com/ and DIY Themes, "The Thesis Statement," http://diythemes.com/thesis/ and StudioPress, "Genesis Framework," http://my.studiopress.com/themes/genesis/.

9. Check out the free Google Web Fonts (https://www.google.com/webfonts) as an example font repository.

10. Patrick Cox, "Developing Balance in Web Design," *Codrops* (blog), September 13, 2011, http://tympanus.net/codrops/2011/09/13/developing-balance-in-web-design/.

11. 960 Grid System, http://960.gs/.

Chapter Seven

An Introduction to Plugins and Media

N ow that you know how to set up and create your own pages and posts, you may want to embellish your website. This chapter looks at how to expand your website's functions by adding plugins and media. WordPress supports adding images, audio, and videos, and embedding files on your website.

PLUGINS

Plugins are bits of code that the creator has packaged together to be imported into a self-hosted WordPress installation to add specific functionalities. A new function may be something such as a calendar, a way to pull in tweets or Flickr photos, or a simple way to accomplish a task that can be done basically within WordPress but would require advanced technical knowledge. The online community has open-sourced thousands of plugins for practically anything you would like to do with WordPress.

Finding, installing, activating, and customizing plugins is nearly identical to the same process in each case for themes. It should be noted that too many plugins can slow a website down, as additional plugins bloat the site's code. When a website visitor comes to your site not only do they have to wait on the core WordPress files to load—plus the theme—but then they also have to wait for all those plugins. Therefore it is a good idea to keep your number of plugins to a minimum—and when possible, to find a way to use WordPress's native capabilities to add additional features to your site.

My recommendation is to first try out a plugin to see how satisfied you are with the results. Then search online for code that will allow you to edit your theme to accomplish the same thing. The drawback of editing a theme is that you will need to remember to make these changes to each new theme you implement. However, if you are using a child theme, then this problem is alleviated somewhat.

In this book I highlight the plugins used on the surveyed libraries' websites. You will find a complete list of described plugins in appendix C. Keep in mind that there are dozens of plugins for nearly any task that you wish to accomplish. The plugins listed in this book are only a suggestion for a particular task and are compatible with the latest version of WordPress as of this writing.

A warning: you should download free plugins only from the official WordPress .org directory, because they have been verified as safe to use.

68

What to Look for in a Plugin

You can learn a lot about a plugin just by visiting its home page on the plugin directory.[1] Plugin developers are encouraged to describe the plugin, how to install it, create a frequently asked questions page, optionally provide other notes, and keep track of changes. The more documentation a plugin has, the more confident you can feel about it and the commitment the creator has to maintaining it. Some plugins offer scarce information but have links to the creator's personal site. There is nothing wrong with this method, but you should scope out the documentation provided offsite before using the plugin.

WordPress does not let plugin creators have all the say in informing the community about their plugin—some automatic information is gathered and presented on each plugin's page as well. This data includes statistics on how many times the plugin has been downloaded, how many versions have appeared, and how actively each version is used by the community; a support forum where users can ask the creator questions; a list of reviews; and finally, the version history of the plugin. While you are looking at a plugin's rating and compatibility, it is also a good idea to check out the support forum. Look to see if the plugin developer has responded to any help requests. Each plugin's home page will list how many questions have been resolved recently. However, the forum is not the end-all of how good a plugin is. The questions posted may be inane or repetitive.

Which WordPress Installations Support Plugins

The three flavors of WordPress differ in their plugin options. The hosted WordPress .com websites cannot install plugins. Instead they have a wide variety of widgets that give some customization and feature options. These widgets are a curated collection of functions that WordPress.com sites support. (We will learn more about widgets later in this chapter.) Multisite networks of blogs can have plugins. However, the variety of plugins is determined by the ones installed by the multisite administrator. Any single website can choose to use or ignore the available plugins. In this way, a multisite is similar to a WordPress.com website.

Therefore, the only flavor of WordPress that has free choice regarding which of the thousands of plugins to indulge in is the self-hosted website. If there were no limits on how many plugins a web server could manage in a fast manner, the site administrator could have an indefinite number of plugins. However, as described above, this is not the case—so be smart about how many plugins you install.

69

How to Find Plugins

Go to the plugins directory (http://wordpress.org/extend/plugins/). Like themes, submitted plugins have various strengths and weaknesses. A plugin may add a cool new function to your site, such as a calendar with multiple display options, but could come at the cost of being bloated with extra lines of code. Those extra lines of code starts to weigh down your site, causing it to load slower. Remember, people have short attention spans, so they will abandon a slow website without hesitation. Each plugin can be rated and commented on by the community. Other users can also leave vote on the compatibility of the plugin with a version of WordPress. You can search by keyword or by tag.

There are also some premium plugins available. These plugins are not available to download through the official website because they do not follow the open source rules. Before you purchase a premium plugin, do some independent research to verify that the plugin is safe and the developer is reputable.

How to Install Plugins

The process for installing a plugin to your website is identical to installing a theme. First, you can download a plugin directly to your computer and then upload it through your dashboard interface. Or you can browse for plugins from within your dashboard, as described above, and then just click to download and activate your choice. Finally, you can upload plugins via the plugins directory on your server. Once your plugin is installed, activate it by going to the dashboard and clicking on Plugins; you will then see all the plugins available for your website. Simply click Activate underneath the plugin that you would like to use on your site.

SHORTCODES

Since WordPress 2.5, nontechnical users have been able to add dynamic content to their posts and pages without needing to know programming. What you do is write a short phrase between square brackets, and WordPress inserts whatever dynamic content should be in that location when the post or page loads. These phrases are known as shortcodes. An example shortcode is *[gallery]*, which you would add to the body of your post or page. When the post or page is saved and you view the live content, you will see a gallery of thumbnail images appear. Each shortcode will need additional parameters so it will know *which* gallery to display, as each gallery has its own ID number. Fortunately, shortcodes are well documented, so it is easy to experiment with adding dynamic content without needing to know PHP.

Shortcodes can also be created by plugins. The Mingle Forums plugin gives you the ability to turn any page on your website into a forum.[2] Once this plugin is activated, you just add the shortcode *[mingleforum]* to the page. Then, in the plugin's settings, you can make adjustments to the forum's functionality—all without digging into any code.

WordPress.com has its own shortcodes list.[3]

Check appendix C for more resources.

ADDING MEDIA

Adding media files to your WordPress website is very simple. Below the title box and above the body box where you enter your content is the Add Media button. The button includes icon of a camera and a musical note. Clicking on this upload button opens a pop-up screen where you can choose how to add your media to your post or page. You can upload files here, add the file by its URL, or choose a file previously uploaded to your media library. Your file can be anything from a video, image, or audio file to a PDF—and more. If your web server has low CPU (i.e., processing power), larger files may not upload or may have small file-size limitations.

Upload Files via Browser

You can upload one file or multiple files at once. Starting in the 3.5 version of WordPress, you can drag and drop a file from your computer to the Media Library. In order for this feature to work, you will need an up-to-date web browser such as Chrome or Firefox. If the drag and drop feature does not work, you can click on Upload Files for a more traditional pop-up window that allows you to select your file to upload. If you have previously uploaded files, you can click on the Media Library link to search for the file to insert into your post or page.

If your file exists elsewhere on the web, you can paste the URL to the content by clicking on the Insert from URL link. There is a danger in linking to files if the file is hosted by someone else because they may take it down at any time, thus leaving your website with a broken file link.

Upload Files via Server

You can also upload themes, plugins, and media to your WordPress website via the server where WordPress is installed. This method is handy for larger files that keep timing out with an error message that the upload is taking long but that you would still like to offer for download. To upload files in this way, open your preferred FTP software and enter your server information (i.e., host, username, and password), then navigate to your WordPress directory. Clicking on the wp-content folder will take you to the directories where your themes, plugins, and media are stored.

This FTP option should be restricted to the administrator of the website since a careless hand may crash your entire website.

File Options

WordPress gives you a number of options to increase your file's accessibility for users with screen readers. Each uploaded file can have a title, alternative text (which appears when the user hovers over an image), a caption, and a description. You can find these fields in the right sidebar. By filling in as many of these fields as possible, your site will be more useful for those with low vision. You can also make selections about how your image is aligned in the post or page. You can also choose how large you want the image to appear on your site. The final option is to set where your media links to. Your options are to link to a special attachment page that keeps your site's appearance but embeds just your file on it (and not the text content or other media); directly to the file; to a custom URL (great for linking to another website); or to nowhere at all.

Images

Image Editing

Once your image is uploaded, you will see a link under the thumbnail (i.e., a very small version of your image), called Edit Image. Clicking on this button will give you a rudimentary set of edit tools. You can do a basic image crop, rotation, flip, and scaling. However, you will achieve the best results by editing your images before you upload them to WordPress.[4]

Create a Gallery

If you want to create an image gallery, you can do that as well via the Add Media button. First, click on the Insert Media link. Then you can search or browse for previously uploaded images. Next, click on the images you want to add to your gallery. A check box will appear on the image. Then click on the Insert into Post button. When you preview your post, your gallery will show up as a series of thumbnails with captions (if the image has a caption). How the image is displayed once clicked upon depends on your theme, settings, and plugins.

Featured Images

Your theme may offer a featured image option. This feature is handy if your post or page has several images in it and you want to designate one image as the primary one. Then when your post is shown in different configurations across the website (e.g., home page, archives, search listing), the featured image will be the one shown for the post or page. To set your featured image via the Add Media button, just click on the Set Featured Image link, then click on the image; finish up by clicking Set Featured Image. A second way to set a featured image—if your theme supports it—is by looking for a widget in your right sidebar called Featured Image when you are creating your post or page. You just click on that widget's link to get started.

Audio

Self-Hosted WordPress Site

In a hosted WordPress website, you can upload an audio file as you would do any other media type. Once it is uploaded, you can edit the file's title, caption, description, and where the file links. Once it is published, a link appears on the post or page. If the link just connects to the media file's location, clicking on the link brings up a black screen with a small audio player in the middle of the screen. There are also plugins that you can use to manage your audio, and a tutorial on ThemeFuse gives some additional options on how to style the audio player.[5]

WordPress.com Site

For WordPress.com users, you have four ways to add audio to your website. The first method is to use a shortcode that links to the music file, which is hosted elsewhere. The shortcode will produce a pretty audio player. Second is to use the hosted-only Playlist Editor to upload and display playlists. This features requires a paid upgrade. You upload your audio files to your website, arrange the songs into the desired order for your playlist, and then add your playlist to your post. Third is to create a download link for a file that is hosted elsewhere; users can click on this link to access the file to listen to it on their own computer. Similar to the default hosted behavior, there is no pretty audio player on the screen. The final option is to embed the SoundCloud Audio Player widget. More detailed instructions for this last option can be found on the WordPress.com website.[6]

Video

URL Method

Videos are crowd favorites on the Web. They are eye catching and a great way to ensure that your message's tone and personality are not lost in translation. WordPress makes it easy to embed videos right into your page or post. The quick way to do it is to copy your video's URL and then paste it on a separate line in your post or page. (Be sure to not put anything else on that line.) Then preview your page. If your video does not show up, you may need to switch to the HTML tab for your body instead of using the Visual Editor. Also, it's not just videos that can be embedded into your content using just the URL. Therefore be sure to check the WordPress Codex article.[7]

Upload and Plugins

For self-hosted sites, if you upload a file via the Media Library, it will act just like an uploaded audio file, with just a link to the content. The video will not display in the page. The Video Embed & Thumbnail Generator plugin gives you a way to embed your uploaded videos right in your post or page.[8] You can even choose which thumbnail to display for the video.

73

On a WordPress.com site, you can use the VideoPress upgrade to upload videos to your website.[9] You will then have the option to edit the video's title. Videos can then be added to the page via a shortcode or by clicking on the Insert into post button. The two special features of VideoPress are that you have access to your video's statistics and you never have to worry about going over your bandwidth.

Embedded Files

An embedded file works the exact same way: by pasting its URL in the content box. A number of popular online services are supported, such as Flickr, Instagram, Scribd, and Twitter. WordPress is adding support for new services all the time, so be sure to check back regularly.[10]

NOTES

1. WordPress.org, "Plugins Directory," http://wordpress.org/extend/plugins/.
2. cartpauj, "Mingle Forum," http://wordpress.org/extend/plugins/.
3. WordPress.com, "Shortcodes," http://en.support.wordpress.com/shortcodes/.
4. I recommend Pixlr Editor (http://pixlr.com/editor) for image editing in your browser.
5. Karol K., "How to Add Audio (Music) to a WordPress Site," 2012, http://themefuse .com/blog/how-to-add-audio-music-to-a-wordpress-site/.
6. WordPress.com, "Audio," http://en.support.wordpress.com/audio/.
7. WordPress.org, "Embeds," http://codex.wordpress.org/Embeds.
8. Kyle Gilman, "Video Embed & Thumbnail Generator," http://wordpress.org/extend/ plugins/video-embed-thumbnail-generator/.
9. WordPress.com, "VideoPress," http://en.support.wordpress.com/videopress/.
10. WordPress.org, "Okay, So What Sites Can I Embed From?" http://codex.wordpress .org/Embeds#Okay.2C_So_What_Sites_Can_I_Embed_From.3F.

Chapter Eight

Administrative Tools

To master WordPress, you need to learn how to use its other CMS features. In this chapter you will learn about how to arrange your workflow, build your information architecture, add functions through widgets, manage users, and add interactivity—and how to keep your website in good working order.

WORKFLOW

The point of a CMS is to make your life considerably easier when building and maintaining a website. It's a time-consuming process to devise a complete website from scratch. Therefore to get the most out of a CMS requires some preplanning. Once you have set up your information architecture and know what content your website is going to have, you need to figure out who can write content, who can edit and publish content, who makes sure that content is always up to date, and whether there are any editors who check all content before it goes up.

Built-in Functions

Each post and page on your website has its own visibility controls. You can decide if a post is available to the public, is private (can be seen only by the logged-in writer), or is password protected. The last option is great for a website where you want to create a members-only section. Each post or page can then have its own password. Content can also be scheduled to be published at the exact date and time that you specify.

If you need to bulk-edit content, you can do that from the All Posts or All Pages menus located in the left sidebar. First, check off the posts or pages that need to be edited. Then look for the Bulk Actions drop-down menu (just above the post listings). By clicking on the arrow, you can then select Edit before clicking Apply. You can now assign the selected content to new categories, change the assigned author (great for sites where the writer has left the organization), turn comments on and off, reassign the workflow status, allow your post to ping (i.e., notify) other sites that your content links to their website, and finally, whether the content should be made "sticky" (i.e., to stay at the top of all pages where that content is displayed).

Finally, all posts or pages on your website have only three workflow states: draft, pending review, or published. As webmaster and WordPress developer Curtiss Grymala points out, there is no practical difference between draft and pending review, since the editors are not automatically notified that a post is ready for review.[1] Fortunately, the WordPress community has stepped in to help improve workflow control.

Plugins

The Edit Flow plugin gives you an editorial calendar, the ability to receive notifications of the workflow progress, a way to manage your writers, and more.[2] The WP Document Revisions plugin allows a user to assign documents to a workflow step and associate the document with a department.[3] The saved document, once opened through the dashboard, remains locked as long as the WordPress page is open—and thus prevents others from working on the same document. While content can be scheduled for publication, there is no built-in function that allows you to configure when content will unpublish or move itself to a new category. For example, you may want a post on the front page for one week and then have it automatically retire to the archive category. The Post Expirator plugin gives you the ability to automatically unpublish posts.[4] Content can be reset as a draft or deleted; it can also be moved to a new category.

NAVIGATION

Your navigational structure determines how users know where they are on your website and how to find other sections. The main clues are through menus, but

76

users can also discover new content through categories and tags. There are many different ways to display navigational elements on your website. The below text includes a few examples of where and when you may want to display navigation on your website.

Menus

The main navigational items of a website link to areas such as "Home," "Catalog," "Services," or "Blog." On most websites, these top-level pages are the primary navigation and are usually found at the top of the website. However, this primary navigation can also appear on the left (the next most popular option), right, or bottom of the page. In countries that read right-to-left, you would expect a sidebar menu to appear on the right. You can also repeat the menu in any two locations. Depending on your theme, you may have only particular spots available to accommodate a menu, but you can also customize your theme to place a menu wherever you like on the page.

You can have more than one menu on a website. Secondary menus may include links that users do not need to navigate or to see all content. These links may include "About," "Contact Us," "Terms of Service," and other pages. WordPress can automatically create menus based on page or post hierarchy; you can also create custom menus if you are bringing together a diverse set of content.[5] Say you have an "About" page for your town library. The main content on this page discusses the history of your library, who the director is, major milestones, and so on. In the sidebar menu, you may want to include links to the town hall, the chamber of commerce, schools, and the like. These custom menus are handled under the Appearance menu on the dashboard.

For WordPress.com websites, you also go to the Appearance menu.[6]

Categories

Your posts can be added to categories, as previously discussed on page 46. Depending upon your theme, your post's categories may appear on the website. By clicking on a category link, a visitor goes to a page listing all the other posts on your website that are in this category. As the site administrator, you can also add categories to your navigational menu. The simplest way would be to create a custom menu item with a URL of /category/mycategory. Also in the Menu settings, you can simply choose to create a custom menu of specific categories that you select. You may want to do this, for example, if you have a Database category with subcategories based on different subjects. You could then set the custom menu so that if the site visitor is looking at your databases, this special Database category listing menu shows up in your sidebar.

Tags

Just like categories, tags work in the same way: when you click on a tag link, you go to a page displaying all posts with that tag. The URL is even similar, though this time it is /*tag/mytag*. Tags are not "smart items"—they do not adjust to different forms of a particular word—so you may want to have a vocabulary dictionary so that everyone only uses the singular or plural version of a word for tags. This way if a post is tagged *cats*, that tag will show all cat-related posts on the website and users will not miss content over in another tag simply called *cat*. (It was also popular a few years ago to display tags in tag cloud menus where the more frequently the tag word was used, the larger it would appear within the menu. However, this display method has fallen by the wayside.)

Page Hierarchy

Pages are organized by parent-child hierarchies, as discussed on page 50. Page hierarchies can be created as a custom menu and placed on the website. Another option is to use the page widget, which allows you to sort pages by title, order, or ID. Widgets are discussed in the "Widgets" section.

PERMALINKS

The links of your website should in general be unchangeable and easy for humans to read. The term for these permanent URLs is *permalinks*. If you want to make your website as friendly as possible, you will want human-friendly permalinks for your posts and pages. By default, WordPress uses a machine-friendly URL that looks like *www.example.com/?p=111*. While this URL is short, it does not tell me much about what the content on this post or page is about. A more reader-friendly option would be *www.example.com/contact*. The idea being that when you are doing tech support over the phone for a patron, you can tell them to go to www.mylibrary .com/reference instead of trying to read to them a long string of letters and numbers. WordPress refers to these more human-friendly URLs as Pretty Permalinks.[7]

On a hosted WordPress website, you can change the URL settings by going to the Settings menu, then clicking on Permalinks. In order to enable Pretty Permalinks, you will need an Apache web server with the mod_rewrite module installed.[8] If you are not able to get Pretty Permalinks working, please contact your server provider or search the WordPress forums.

A variety of URL options are available to you, but the basic parts you can add are the date, post name, or category. You can also create a custom URL structure that may, for example, mix the date and name of the post.[9] All this goes back to being careful in how you name your site's categories—be consistent and helpful to your users. By using one-word categories, your website's URLs will be shorter and neater for it. WordPress also recognizes parent and child categories, so by just including the category tag once in your custom URL structure, the parent and child categories display in your URL.

Examples of custom URL structures:

- /%year%/%monthnum%/%day%/%postname%/
  comes out as
  2016/12/27/wordpress-basics/
- /%category%/%postname%/
  comes out as
  /databases/heritagequest/
- /%author%/%year%/
  comes out as
  /agoodman/2016/

There is also an advanced method of creating your permalinks. You can create a new custom post and use custom fields, as explained in a Rhys Wynne article.[10] Using a custom post type and field could create a database post type that has custom field for a particular discipline. For example, your custom permalink could be /databases/humanities/. In this case, databases is your custom post type and humanities is a custom field. Wynne's article gives you the technical specs for achieving this effect. This is a similar method to just using parent-child categories.

If your website is mostly pages, you probably do not want to include dates in your URLs. However, for blogs, it is a good idea to have dates in your URLs so you and your users know when a post was written. Remember that posts are usually about time-sensitive information, such as next week's movie marathon. Another tip is that if you are displaying the content's title in the URL, try to keep your titles to five words and under to keep the URLs short. A long title may wrap to the second line on the post which may mess up your site's appearance. If you share your site's posts or pages on Twitter, also consider a URL shortening service (such at bitly, mentioned above). To learn more about sharing your site's links on social media, please see the "Website Planning: Analytics" section.

For WordPress.com websites, the URL structure cannot be changed.

WIDGETS

Many websites have one or more sidebars next to the main content on the page. In WordPress, these sidebars are where you place a wide variety of functions, called widgets. How many sidebars your website has to place widgets in depends upon the theme installed. The areas on a theme where widgets can be placed may also include the footer or even the header.

So what are widgets, exactly? They are additional functions that can display a list of pages, a calendar, tag clouds, links, HTML code, and so on. There are a number of widgets that come with WordPress by default and more that can be added via plugins. The example given earlier—of placing a custom menu about town resources such as the chamber of commerce and town hall on a library's "About" page—could instead be created through a links widget.

New widgets can be found and installed on self-hosted installations as with plugins; the new widget appears in your Available Widgets box. WordPress.com websites have access only to the widgets already provided.

Add a Widget

To get started testing widgets on your website, go to the Appearance menu and then click on Widgets. If your theme supports widgets, you should see an area to the far right that may already have some widgets preplaced. In another tab in your web browser, go to your website's front page to see if you can match the preplaced widgets with your front page. For default WordPress installations, you will usually see an Archive and Meta widget, which includes the log-in/log-out link. Try left-clicking on one of the widgets back in the dashboard and drag it to the left to either the Available or Inactive Widgets box (the Inactive area will save the settings for that widget in case you decide to use it again). Now drag the Text widget from the Available Widgets area to a widget location on the right. Once placed, the widget opens up and gives you the opportunity to title it, plus a place to add some additional text. For this exercise, add the title "Hello"; in the text box, type "Welcome to my website!" Then click the Save button on the bottom left and the Close link on the bottom right.

View Your Widget

View your site's front page to see the widget. If you do not see it, your theme may be set up so that some widget locations show up only on specific areas of the website, such as the "Archives" page. The point of this exercise is to just get used to the idea of adding, changing, and moving widgets around so you know where they display on your website.

Control Where Widgets Appear

Setting up widgets is very simple and is a great way to enrich your website with additional information, photo streams from Flickr, and the like. However, you need a way to control that a particular widget shows up only on particular pages or posts on your website. Plugins come to the rescue here too! A great post by Alexandra Samuel gives you a rundown on the different plugin options for widget control.[11] You may need to try out several plugins till you find one that makes sense for your website.

USERS

In a general sense, a user is a person who visits your website. Usually your visitors will be a silent majority who pop in to read or view your content and then leave without comment. However, a user may also refer to someone who is a member of your website. This user may or may not be actively contributing content. You can allow people to join your website under the Settings menu then in General. Simply check the box next to Membership. You can then assign new members a default role on your website. You may also elect to add new members yourself through the Users menu—which is also the only way to add users on a WordPress.com website.

Roles

WordPress comes with five default roles: subscriber, administrator, editor, author, and contributor. WordPress.com does not have a subscriber role. Each role is assigned permissions for what a user of that role can do on the website. For example, the administrator can control all aspects of the website from the theme to managing other users while an author can only post new content. More information on roles and permissions can be found on the Codex.[12]

If the defaults are too narrow for your user management needs, you can install plugins to add or edit roles, such as user role editor.[13] While making user management decisions, be sure to think carefully about what you want each user to be able to do. Users who can publish their own content on your website will need to have their content supervised just in case their account is ever taken over by someone with malicious intent. You could end up with spam or damaging content published that to the casual viewer may seem legitimate.

Profiles

Each person who has an account on your website will have a profile. This small bit of personal space allows the user to specify their name, nickname, contact information, and even a little biographical information. By default these profiles are not readily available to site visitors for hosted WordPress websites since clicking on a writer's name only takes you to a list of posts by them. However, there are plugins that can display a list of users on your website, such as WordPress Users.[14] If you are an advanced user, you can also create your own author template where you can code a way to display profiles.[15] For WordPress.com users, profiles are automatically available to the public.[16]

Customize the Dashboard

With a bit of work, you can also customize the appearance of the dashboard. There are two main ways of customizing the dashboard. First, you can edit your theme's PHP files to remove widgets entirely or to appear based upon a user's role.[17] Second, you could look for a plugin such as WP Total Hacks.[18] This plugin allows you to customize your dashboard's logo, edit the footer text, remove widget boxes, and more.

For a nonadministrator, unnecessary widgets on the dashboard can be confusing. For example, the WordPress news widgets take up a lot of real estate and can be distracting. Is the editor supposed to know something about the latest WordPress news? Should they tell someone? As a good rule of thumb, you should eliminate as much of the distraction as possible for your internal users.

There are other ways you can enhance a user's internal interaction with the login screen and dashboard. For instance, having a consistent brand on your website is important. You can customize the login screen through the Erident Custom Login and Dashboard plugin.[19] By changing the login screen, you can keep a more consistent look to your site and not confuse users as to why they are logging into WordPress instead of *your* site. As the administrator of your website, you may want to see a history of all the activity on the site. The Simple History plugin will place a widget on your dashboard to show who has posted new content or activated new plugins.[20] If your workflow allows it, you can also use the Dashboard Notepad plugin to leave notes to users of certain roles.[21] For example, you can leave a note telling editors that the website will be updated this weekend. These plugins are just the beginning of how you can personalize the dashboard for your needs.

INTERACTIVITY

One of the best benefits of WordPress is being able to interact with your visitors. Below are the three main ways to get interactivity and feedback from users.

Comments

WordPress's greatest interactivity strength is in its comment settings. Comments can usually be found on the posts of a website but not the pages. To get started, go to the Settings menu, then click on Discussion. You have the power to decide if comments are allowed on your website and if so, whether they need approval before being posted or whether they need to be marked as spam if there are too many links in the comment. If you have the Akismet plugin installed and configured, a lot of the work of monitoring for spam comments is taken off your shoulders. The comments section can also be set to close after a specific length of time so people are not commenting on ancient posts. However, the real power is further down the page, where you can blacklist certain words (AKA foul language), users, IP addresses, or e-mail addresses from ever appearing on your website. (This capability should ease the concerns of stakeholders who fear that allowing comments will lead to a bunch of bad words appearing on your website!)

You can easily see how many new comments have been left on your website when you first log in. Comment counts are posted on the top bar, on the dashboard, and in the left menu. You can review comments and reply, delete, or report them as spam.

Forums

By default, there is no forum option rolled into WordPress. However, you can install a plugin on a hosted website to get this functionality. As discussed earlier, Mingle Forum is easy to set up.[22] After you install and activate the plugin, create a new page where the forum can display and add the Mingle Forum shortcode. Then, in the Mingle Forum menu item on the dashboard, set up how many individual forums you want to appear on that page. Users of the forum can create an account and start chatting within minutes.

Share and Social Media Buttons

A popular component of websites is the ability to "like" a post or share it with friends. This interactive option is so popular that there are over a thousand such plugins on WordPress.org. Some themes have social media buttons rolled right into the theme. If you need to install a plugin, you will then need to modify the settings of the plugin to make decisions on what sharing buttons to include on your site and where the buttons will appear on the post. Each plugin will give you different options.

For WordPress.com, sharing buttons are built right into the platform. Under the Settings menu, click on Sharing. You can then decide which social media sites to support, customize how the buttons look, and where the buttons appear on your website. Be aware not overwhelm your site visitors with too many icons—they can become distracting.

WordPress.com Bonus Interactions

You have three extra interactivity features built in if you are using WordPress.com for your website. The first is to insert a poll and requires a Polldaddy.com account (which has free registration). The free version allows two hundred survey responses per month, so it is very limited. The second feature is the ability to create a form. You decide which fields to include and then add the form to your post. Responses can be viewed through the Feedbacks link on the dashboard. Third, you can share your work with others to get feedback before you publish your content. On the post and page edit screen, just click on the Request Feedback button. Then enter the e-mail addresses of the person when you would like to review your content and customize the message the person receives about your request. If e-mail is not your thing, you can also just copy a URL to send to your reviewer.

UPDATES AND UPGRADES

As stated earlier, to keep your website secure, you need to keep your website updated. What this means is making sure that your WordPress core, themes, and plugins are the latest version. Updates fix bugs, security loopholes, and add new features. An *upgrade* refers to a major new version of WordPress.

Updating your WordPress website is very easy through the use of subtle but persistent "nag screens." You will see two arrows following each other in a circle along the top bar of your website and a number in a dark circle in your left sidebar once you are logged in. The easier way to get your updates is to click the button in the top bar; you then can select what you want to update before hitting Update. While updating, WordPress puts your site on maintenance mode so anyone visiting your site will see a brief "be right back" notice. This update process usually only takes a few seconds, but you still should probably run the updates at night or when your traffic is low.

While WordPress is great at updating automatically, you can never be sure whether the new update will break something on your website. Therefore it is recommended to run the updates on your development server first to check for incompatibility issues.

BACKUP AND MIGRATION

Because you will spend a lot of hours working on your website setting up, filling it with content, and then maintaining it, you want to make sure your site's database is backed up. The database contains "every post, every comment and every link" on your website.[23] It is important that you back up often and save your backups in different locations. Ideally, one of your backup locations would be located offsite, such as in the cloud. The point is if your library burned down taking your server room with it—your website's backup would exist across campus or on another site.

Backing Up a Self-Hosted WordPress Database

The WordPress Codex includes several methods for backing up your site. Some options include having your webhost back up your site or copying your files to your computer. You can also manually log into your phpMyAdmin database to export a copy of your data as well. Check out the codex for their suggestions.[24]

Another simple backup system is to use a plugin. My favorite backup plugin is called WordPress Database Backup (WP-DB-Backup).[25] Simply install the plugin, and then go through the Tools menu to Backup to adjust the settings. You can have your backup saved to your server (not the safest option), download it to your computer, or have the backup e-mailed to you (what I choose). Then set how often you want the backup to take place. I have my backup e-mailed to me daily with a filter on my e-mail so that the backup is immediately archived without cluttering my inbox. If you then need to restore your database, you can import your backup through phpMyAdmin.

There are other backup plugins available. More information can be found on the WordPress Codex.

Backing Up Posts and Pages through Export

WordPress.com websites are limited in backup options since you cannot install plugins or access the backend of the website. However, both WordPress.org and WordPress.com websites have an Export feature. You will be able to export only your post and page content. (This means you will leave behind comments and links.) To use Export, log in to your website and click on Tools, then Export for a XML file. You probably want to export all content; next, click on Download Export File. This file can then be imported into another WordPress website.

Backing Up Other Content

Media, plugins, and themes will not be in the database backup or the export file. They will need to be copied from the server for self-hosted websites. For WordPress .com, an option to download your media files only appears if you are migrating your content to a WordPress.com website or to a self-hosted WordPress website.[26]

Migration

Moving a WordPress website is not too difficult. The following is an overview of the process: download your database and export your content through the Export function. (Make sure to grab your media, plugins, and themes folders as well.) On your new server, install WordPress. Next, import the WordPress database through phpMyAdmin, then import your XML file under the Tools menu. Finally, copy your media, plugins, and themes files to their folders on the new server.

WordPress.org has more information about how to deal with domain or URL changes and moving a multisite installation.[28] If you are migrating a WordPress.com to another hosted website or your own hosted version, see the "Support" page.[29]

NOTES

1. Curtiss Grymala, "Adding a Bit of Workflow to WordPress," 2011, http://www .centernetworks.com/workflow-wordpress/.

2. Mohammad Jangda, Daniel Bachhuber, Scott Bressler, and automattic, "Edit Flow," http://wordpress.org/extend/plugins/edit-flow/.

3. Benjamin J. Balter, "WP Document Revisions," http://wordpress.org/extend/plugins/ wp-document-revisions/.

4. Aaron Axelsen, "Post Expirator," http://wordpress.org/extend/plugins/post-expirator/.

5. Ed Andrea, "Using WordPress Custom Menus," 2012, http://www.ostraining.com/ blog/wordpress/using-wordpress-custom-menus/.

6. WordPress.com, "Custom Menus," http://en.support.wordpress.com/menus/.

7. WordPress.org, "Using Permalinks," http://codex.wordpress.org/Using_Permalinks.

8. WordPress.org, "Using "Pretty" permalinks," http://codex.wordpress.org/Using _Permalinks#Using_.22Pretty.22_permalinks.

9. WordPress.org, "Structure Tags," http://codex.wordpress.org/Using_Permalinks #Structure_Tags.

10. Rhys Wynne, "Advanced WordPress SEO: Add Custom Values to Permalinks Through Custom Fields and Posts," 2012, http://3doordigital.com/custom-fields-and-posts-in -wordpress-permalink-urls/.

11. Alexandra Samuel, "Choosing a widget control plugin for WordPress," http://www .alexandrasamuel.com/toolbox/choosing-a-widget-control-plugin-for-wordpress.

12. WordPress.org, "Roles and Capabilities," http://codex.wordpress.org/Roles_and _Capabilities.

13. Vladimir Garagulya, "User Role Editor," http://wordpress.org/extend/plugins/user -role-editor/.

14. jonkemp, "WordPress Users," http://wordpress.org/extend/plugins/wordpress-users/.

15. WordPress.org, "Author Templates," http://codex.wordpress.org/Author_Templates.

16. WordPress.com, "User Profile," http://en.support.wordpress.com/user-profile/.

17. Connor Turnball, "12 Useful Customization and Branding Tweaks for the WordPress Dashboard," 2011, http://wp.tutsplus.com/articles/12-useful-customization-and -branding-tweaks-for-the-wordpress-dashboard/.

18. Takayuki Miyauchi, "WP Total Hacks," http://wordpress.org/extend/plugins/wp-total-hacks/.

19. Libin V. Babu, "Erident Custom Login and Dashboard," http://wordpress.org/extend/plugins/erident-custom-login-and-dashboard/.

20. Pär Thernstrom, "Simple History," http://wordpress.org/extend/plugins/simple-history/.

21. Stephanie Leary, "Dashboard Notepad," http://wordpress.org/extend/plugins/dashboard-notepad/. Be sure to check out Leary's other plugins on her profile page: http://profiles.wordpress.org/sillybean/.

22. cartpauj, "Mingle Forum," http://wordpress.org/extend/plugins/mingle-forum/.

23. WordPress.org, "WordPress Backups," http://codex.wordpress.org/WordPress_Backups.

24. Ibid.

25. Austin Matzko, "WP-DB-Backup," http://wordpress.org/extend/plugins/wp-db-backup/.

26. WordPress.org, "Restoring Your Database from Backup," http://codex.wordpress.org/Restoring_Your_Database_From_Backup.

27. WordPress.com, "Moving a Blog," http://en.support.wordpress.com/moving-a-blog/.

28. WordPress.org, "Moving WordPress," http://codex.wordpress.org/Moving_WordPress.

29. Ibid.

3

PART 3

Library Implementations of WordPress

Chapter Nine

Academic Libraries

PARKS LIBRARY PRESERVATION

http://parkslibrarypreservation.wordpress.com

The Parks Library Preservation website provides backstage access into the Library & Archives Preservation Department at Iowa State University Library. Since many library websites focus on events and new materials, it is refreshing to see how a less visible library department works. The Parks website was built to work within the restraints of a hosted WordPress.com website. However, the free website has not limited the impact the department makes on educating the community about preservation.

The full range of WordPress.com's built-in features is used on the Parks website. The main content area consists of the default chronological posts from using WordPress like a blog as you can see in the screen shot (fig. 9.1). Each post includes large photos that have been uploaded through the Media Library. Each photo also has a descriptive caption, which improves the site's accessibility. Social sharing links are included to make it easy to share the website's content. Each post is also clearly labeled with multiple categories to allow the reader to seek posts of similar content. Another navigational element is a horizontal menu of static pages across the top of the website. The pages include a great deal of additional depth about preservation techniques, information about staff, and helpful tips for your own preservation efforts. Then in the sidebar are social media, e-mail subscription boxes, and RSS feed links to allow the reader to choose how to keep informed about

FIGURE 9.1
Parks Library Preservation website

Parks Library Preservation's work. Additional links in the sidebar list preservation resources, and other preservation websites. Finally, the website can be searched by keyword, category, or month.

Melissa Tedone, conservator in the Preservation Department at Iowa State University, answered the survey about her department's usage of WordPress.

The Library and Its Users

Iowa State University is located in the rural farmland of Ames, Iowa. The university has the distinction of having built the first electronic digital computer and assisted in producing the atomic bomb as part of the Manhattan Project.[1] Despite these big-name projects, the town of Ames has a population of approximately 55,000, of which 30,000 are students at the university. Parks Library therefore is a "unique and important resource for the local community," Tedone writes.

The library provides support for a wide range of users. The community of students, faculty, staff, alums, scholars, donors, and local population has a wide range of technical capabilities. Some users prefer the telephone over the Internet, according to Tedone, while the university is home to a computer sciences PhD program. The University Library, with its diverse population, must be capable of providing resources to a wide range of users.

Why They Chose WordPress

Academic libraries often do some sort of preservation and conservation techniques in-house. Despite the Parks Library Preservation program being well established, many within the preservation community were unaware of their efforts. Therefore a decision was made to create a blog to raise awareness of the program. Aside from connecting to other professionals, the blog has served as a way to "showcase the unique work we do while providing practical information about preservation to our readers," Tedone writes. Educating the community and raising the department's profile with colleagues is part of the Preservation Department's mission, which WordPress has helped them to achieve.

Permission to create the blog first had to be received from the associate dean, David Gregory. Tedone and her direct supervisor—Hilary Seo, head of the Preservation Department—approached Gregory. With permission granted, Tedone studied other successful preservation blogs to discover the best platform. Tedone writes that WordPress was chosen for the professional templates that were available and its established reputation among academic bloggers. Other attractive features included: spam could be filtered, the site was free to use, and the statistics were easy to understand. Later after the site was launched, Tedone found it easy to modify and expand the website as they thought of new improvements (e.g., new blogs to follow, additional pages). She writes that "we enjoyed the quickness and flexibility of the blogging platform, and it allowed us to experiment and see what worked best." Further decisions about the website are made between Tedone and her supervisor that follow the policies outlined in the library's "Social Media Working Group Report & Recommendations."

Building with WordPress

The Preservation Department trusts the WordPress.com platform for their website outreach. The department set aside no funding for building a website, so the free blog and theme has allowed them an online presence at no cost. The website was then quick to launch, working within the limited but beautiful space of a free WordPress.com account.

Tedone launched the website after only a month of research and experimenting with the platform.

While no direct money is budgeted specifically for the website, Tedone's job duties have been modified to include maintaining the website and the department's social media presence. Together these activities are considered part of her outreach duties, she reports. The other Perseveration Department staff was encouraged to contribute to the blog, but 80 percent of the posts were being written by Tedone two years after the site's launch. It was then decided that all members of the department would be required to contribute a post. Since the site updates on Tuesdays, a publication scheduled was devised for six months in advance giving staff ample time to prepare their posts. Tedone writes that this additional participation has cut her writing responsibilities in half. Staff are asked to submit their posts to her on the Friday before so she can edit and make sure that items such as photos are showing up in the post.

For backup, the Preservation Departments takes a two-pronged approach. First, they rely on WordPress to manage the backups. Then every two years they print out a physical copy of the blog using the Blog2Print website service.[2] The printed copy of the blog is then added to the department's reference collection.

Evaluation

The blog is meeting the department's outreach and educational needs. Site metrics for page views, how long people are on the site, and so on are collected through WordPress.com's StatCounter. Feedback is gathered online through e-mail and comments on the department's social media website and offline through word of mouth. Suggestions from the community are taken seriously. For example, a request came in for more posts on digital topics, so "we have increased the number of posts assigned to our Digital Initiatives Unit staff," Tedone writes. Department staff receive a monthly social media report that describes how the website is doing. Staff are then able to see the impact of their work, as Tedone highlights other websites that have shared and blogged about the staff's contributed posts.

One of the major goals of establishing the blog was to raise awareness of the work that the Preservation Department is doing. Outreach has been successful, and currently the department writes a series of collaborative posts with the Preservation Department at Duke University Libraries.[3] Tedone writes that "the blog [has made] us more visible within our profession"—all of which was done using a free web publishing platform!

Special Features

Two of the three special features of this website deal with the content of the website itself. First, each blog post contains images that illustrate the work of the staff. Tedone writes that staff are encouraged to use photos to document their work while also following "the philosophy that a picture is worth a thousand words when it comes to blogging." Second, the Preservation Department shares their internal list of equipment vendors on the website. This generosity of sharing previously private information can assist other conservationists in their own work.

The third special feature is the social media sharing buttons. Interacting with readers through social media is an important part of the department's outreach efforts. Therefore, the ability to share the blog's posts through online services such as StumbleUpon and Pinterest are vital.[4] WordPress.com websites have the ability to share website content built right into the platform. Once logged in, go to the Settings menu, then click on Sharing. Halfway down the page are different sharing buttons that WordPress.com supports. For the Preservation Department's website, they left-clicked on an Available Service and then dragged the desired icon to the Enabled Services box. Then they choose the Button Style of Official Buttons. Next, they choose which content on the website (e.g., pages, posts) should have social media sharing buttons. Finally they hit the Save Changes button. What was once a profession hidden and unknown to the general public is now producing a blog that is getting hits on popular social media. Tedone writes that "members of the general public have started 'pinning' some of our posts to Pinterest, which has resulted in an unexpected boost in blog views." These pins are in turn educating the public about preservation, which is part of the department's mission.

SCHOLARLY PUBLISHING @ MIT LIBRARIES

http://libraries.mit.edu/sites/scholarly/

At the Massachusetts Institute of Technology (MIT) Libraries, WordPress has been used to create an informational hub on open access Scholarly Publishing @ MIT Libraries. Peter Suber, director of the Harvard Open Access Project, describes open-access literature as being free and accessible by anyone who has access to the Internet. Suber also writes that open-access literature may be collected in repositories for all content that is produced by that institution or be part of peer reviewed journals.[5] MIT's Scholarly Publishing website was built to assist faculty and "researchers who have questions about their options and rights in the world of scholarly publishing."[6]

The MIT Libraries uses WordPress to manage and promote many of their projects. For the Scholarly Publishing site, information about open access publishing is gathered together in a format that is easy for faculty and researchers to navigate while exploring their publication options. In addition to pages regarding MIT's open access policies, content is aggregated from websites located outside of the website though the use of RSS feeds. The site also includes podcasts and videos about scholarly publishing. Across the top of the home page is a slider highlighting four aspects of the website, as visible in the screen shot (fig. 9.2). Navigation is handled through links that run horizontally across the top of the website, and additional links are located in the right sidebar.

Remlee Green, user experience librarian at MIT Libraries in Cambridge, Massachusetts, answered the survey about her library's usage of WordPress.

The Library and Its Users

MIT Libraries is located in Cambridge, Massachusetts, just west of Boston. The libraries serve a total population of 23,407, including 10,894 students for the 2011–2012 academic year. During this same time period, the website saw 595,407 unique visitors, according to Green. Like many large academic institutions, MIT consists of multiple libraries for a total of six libraries. MIT Libraries also maintains smaller service locations.[7] As part of a highly respected academic community, MIT users of the website are well educated and tech savvy. These users are faculty and graduate students who are writing articles for publications.

FIGURE 9.2
MIT Libraries site

Why They Chose WordPress

Scholarly publishing is a vital part of academic research and professional growth for faculty and researchers. At MIT Libraries, the need to better support and educate their researchers resulted in the creation of the Scholarly Publishing website. With the website in place, the staff was then able to point researchers to a single location to find MIT's policies regarding open access publishing. At MIT, faculty is required to give MIT permission to freely disseminate their research publications when the publications are not restricted by other licensing agreements.[8]

WordPress was chosen for this website because MIT Libraries already use the software for other projects. These other WordPress websites include special projects about MIT history, individual library sites such as MIT Rotch Library, and a site that discusses 150 unique library items, among other websites.[9] Thus, staff was already familiar with the platform and needed little additional training, if any. Green writes that "the option of adding widgets and plug-ins make WordPress an adaptable, low-barrier, low-cost tool for creating websites."

Building with WordPress

Since library staff had already built other WordPress websites, it was decided that the Scholarly Publishing website would be created completely in-house as another aspect of a WordPress Multisite. The User Experience–User Interface Group modified a preexisting WordPress theme, the Station, purchased from WOO Themes for the website.[10] Under this team, the site's navigation was decided, as well as the overall design. The website's content was written by Ellen Duranceau, the program manager for Scholarly Publishing & Licensing. Her guidance ensured that the website met the needs of the users. Altogether, the website took six months to create from the initial idea to launch.

Evaluation

The Scholarly Publishing website seems to be addressing the needs of the targeted user base. Statistics for site usage are tracked by Google Analytics. However, Green writes that "much [of the] assessment for this site is based on qualitative data and hunches about what is or isn't working well."

Special Features

Since the website covers the active and developing areas of open access and copyright, the content on the website cannot remain purely static. Therefore RSS feeds are used to pull in new entries in the right sidebar on the front page of the website. Green explains that the news items are pulled from the Scholarly Publishing category of the MIT Libraries news blog.[11] Meanwhile the DSpace articles are harvested from the MIT Open Access Articles posted to Dspace@MIT.[12]

To keep from coding the tables used on the "Podcasts & Videos" page, the WP-Table Reloaded plugin was utilized.[13] Tables are used on the website for quick layout listings of the podcasts and videos. In modern web design, tables are frowned upon for layouts, but in this case this method is used correctly for data that is best displayed in tables. The WP-Table Reloaded plugin manages tables through the Tools navigation menu in the dashboard. Customization options allow you to choose colors, to export and import tables, and even to use Javascript libraries to sort your tables. For a staff member with minimal coding experience and little time to do the intensive work of coding tables, this plugin can quickly organize data on any website.

ADDITIONAL LIBRARIES

Bates Information & Library Services

www.bates.edu/ils/

This library department has created its own Frequently Asked Questions website. Clicking on the How-to link leads to a tabbed interface. Posts are sorted into categories by topic and are tagged for easier searching.

Digital Public Library of America

http://dp.la/

Centralized information center for ongoing information about the DPLA. Slideshows and a search box are on bottom of the site.

George Mason University Libraries Research Portal

http://library.gmu.edu/portals.html

This landing page leads to discipline-specific research portals. Each portal has customized database search boxes and posts related to new information about that field of study. The theme of each site is slightly different from the others.

Milligan College P.H. Welshimer Memorial Library

http://library.milligan.edu/

This site uses LibraryThing for their rotating slideshow on the front page.[14] Their databases use drop-down menus and CSS3 buttons; a Twitter feed displays in right sidebar. The FAQs are links to posts on a WordPress.com website.

University of South Florida Libraries

www.lib.usf.edu/

This is a highly customized WordPress website. The library uses a lot of widgets, has a slideshow on the front page, has various social media feeds, and uses mega menus for navigation. The special collection section features a description and an image representing the collection. The website's catalog is integrated into the website. Embedded Google Forms are used to collect data.

NOTES

1. Wikipedia, "Iowa State University: Distinctions," http://en.wikipedia.org/wiki/Iowa_State_University#Distinctions.

2. "Blog2Print," http://blog2print.sharedbook.com/blogworld/printmyblog/index.html.

3. Parks Library Preservation, "1091 Project," http://parkslibrarypreservation.wordpress.com/category/1091-project/.

4. StumbleUpon, www.stumbleupon.com; Pinterest, https://pinterest.com/.

5. Berman Center for Internet & Society, "Harvard Open Access Project," http://cyber.law.harvard.edu/research/hoap; Peter Suber, "Open Access Overview," 2012, www.earlham.edu/~peters/fos/overview.htm.

6. Scholarly Publishing @ MIT Libraries, "About," http://libraries.mit.edu/sites/scholarly/about/.

7. MIT Libraries, "Libraries at MIT," http://libraries.mit.edu/about/.

8. Scholarly Publishing @ MIT Libraries, "MIT Faculty Open Access Policy," March 2009, http://libraries.mit.edu/sites/scholarly/mit-open-access/open-access-at-mit/mit-open-access-policy/.

9. MIT Libraries, "MIT History," http://libraries.mit.edu/sites/mithistory/; MIT Libraries, "Rotch Library of Architecture & Planning," http://libraries.mit.edu/sites/rotch/; MIT Libraries, "150 Years in the Stacks," http://libraries.mit.edu/sites/150books/.

10. WOO Themes, "The Station," www.woothemes.com/products/the-station/.

11. MIT Libraries, "MIT Libraries News," http://libraries.mit.edu/sites/news/.

12. DSpace@MIT, "MIT Open Access Articles," http://dspace.mit.edu/handle/1721.1/49433.

13. Tobias Bäthge, "WP-Table Reloaded," http://wordpress.org/extend/plugins/wp-table-reloaded/.

14. LibraryThing, www.librarything.com.

Chapter Ten

Library Associations

ASK A LIBRARIAN DELAWARE STAFF

http://aalstaff.lib.de.us/

The target audience of a library's WordPress website may not be the general public. The Ask a Librarian Delaware Staff website is such a case in that WordPress is used to share information among library staff. Since the network of providers is spread throughout the state, the need to have a centralized location to house materials for service providers shaped the creation of this WordPress website. The virtual reference schedule can be viewed online, and helpful resources are easily accessible to all members. This information hub model is a slicker implementation than a single locked-down computer that is accessible onsite only when the system's virtual reference operators may work from nonlibrary locations.

WordPress meets the requirement for a centralized repository of information for Delaware Libraries' virtual reference services. The website is made up of pages that include helpful shared resources and information about the program. On the home page, a rotating image (called a slider or carousel) highlights news and events (as seen in the screen shot, fig. 10.1), while below items are broken into columns listing the latest announcements, resources for connecting with other staff members, and scheduling information about meetings and training. A link to a separate reference service, QuestionPoint, is located prominently in the left sidebar on all pages. Other interesting information included on the website are chat statistics, marketing and promotional materials, and meeting notes. Additionally,

FIGURE 10.1
Ask a Librarian Delaware site

an embedded Google Calendar lists all staff schedules. Then a ZOHO chat box is embedded on various pages to connect the user to Cathay Crosby, the statewide coordinator of the program. WordPress on this website is helping people connect not only to resources but also to one another through the embedded calendar and chat widget.

Crosby, statewide coordinator of Ask a Librarian Delaware, and Christine Karpovage, web and graphic designer, both work for the Delaware Division of Libraries and answered the survey about their usage of WordPress.

The Library and Its Users

Unlike most other WordPress sites and projects listed in this book, the Ask a Librarian Delaware Staff website's intended audience is library staff members. Crosby writes that these virtual reference personnel come from Delaware academic, public, and special libraries that participate in the program. However, the website at the time of this writing is not locked down, so anyone who visits the site can see which library's staff are manning the virtual desk, view training materials, and have access to online resources that staff use in their work (e.g., a list of helpful websites). The secondary audiences for the website are librarians who are interested in joining the program and library advocates who are looking for virtual reference services. In the future, the website's more sensitive information may be password protected.

It is important that everyone—from the newest staff member to the liaisons who use QuestionPoint—is able to use and navigate the website. QuestionPoint is used to send questions to the patron's home library for further help.[1]

Why They Chose WordPress

Since the centralized sharing of training resources is important to this network of librarians, WordPress is an ideal way to meet these needs. Crosby writes that the ability to post "[information] about upcoming meetings, events, and trainings are also timely and easily posted on this WordPress site." Since Crosby is also working with Maryland's AskUsNow! service, she needed a website that was easy for her to use.[2] The ease of use for maintaining and navigating the website is important for helping to "maintain consistency in service and standards for answering [questions]."[3] The embedded staff schedules also make it easy to see who is covering the online chats without the need to log on to Google Calendar directly.

Two other key players had a part in making decisions about the website. One was Beth-Ann Ryan, the deputy director for the Delaware Division of Libraries, who gave advice on the process. The other person was Karpovage, the Delaware Libraries' web designer. Her previous experience in modifying and rebuilding the main Delaware Libraries' website (http://lib.de.us/) in WordPress assisted her in recommending WordPress for this project.[4] Karpovage then showed Crosby how to use WordPress as well as guided her on "guidelines about the State of Delaware/ DDL's perimeters and expectations for use," Crosby writes.

Building with WordPress

The Ask website took six months to create from conception to implementation. The design is copied from the main Delaware Libraries website. This theme template is a customized version of the "my world with grass and dew" theme by myThemes.[5] Karpovage writes that the website is maintained on a server ran by the state of Delaware, which hosts other state agency websites. When the site's plugins need to be updated, this is handled on a global scale after testing each plugin. It is important to not upgrade or install new plugins without first checking to make sure that the update will not break any other component on the website. Equally vital—especially for a state website—is to ensure that a new plugin will not add a breach to any firewalls and thus compromise all the other websites.

Evaluation

The website is meeting the goal of being a centralized repository very well. New users tell Crosby that the website's resources help them ease the transition from traditional face-to-face reference to online chat. Crosby also notes that because of using WordPress, the number of announcements posted to an electronic discussion list is reduced. As well, those who want the latest information do not need to dig through e-mails but can simply go to the Ask website for a refresher. All the training documentation is stored on the website, making it easy to see the history of the service as it continues to evolve to meet the needs of Delaware residents.

Site statistics are tracked through WordPress's SiteStats. Using this feature, Crosby is able to see which features are most in demand and thus should be moved to a more accessible area of the website. When Crosby does in-person training on the website, she also solicits feedback from new users.

Special Features

The Ask website is built for the greatest ease of use for a very busy professional managing a dispersed network of service providers. Therefore the website needs to be simple to use. For the slideshow on the front of the website, Karpovage chose the Smooth Slider plugin by internet techies.[6] This plugin met the state requirements and did not allow any security breaches in the firewall. (Smooth Slider is a highly customizable plugin that can be embedded to a page using a shortcode or a bit of PHP code, or through a widget. You can choose the posts and which associated image per post shows up in the slider. The plugin is well documented, so adding it to your website is simple to do as long as you are not afraid to poke around in the back end.)

The second plugin the Ask website uses is the All in One SEO Pack plugin.[7] This plugin, as the name suggests, makes a website more search engine friendly through a collection of methods called search engine optimization (SEO). The instructions for enabling this plugin are very simple—it can work right out of the box. If you are more experienced at analyzing your website's search engine results, you can fine-tune this plugin's options to get better results.

PLAINS TO PEAKS POST

http://nnlm.gov/mcr/p2pp/

There are many platforms to provide educational articles to professionals in your field. Journals may exist as physical print mailings, e-mails, or blogs, or as open-access repositories. The National Network of Libraries of Medicine (NN/LM) uses WordPress to create an online journal. The network's online publications are collected at the Plains to Peaks Post (P2PP) website. In a competitive field of access to valuable resources, an open online journal system is a way to ensure equal access to shared knowledge. Medical journals are very expensive even for well-endowed libraries, so open access removes the cost barrier.

WordPress enables the P2PP to present the layout of a traditional journal structure (fig. 10.2) while using the versatility of a website. The left column serves as the table of contents for the current issue with links to individual articles which are listed by title as seen in the screen shot. Previous issues are listed by issue date, which is in month-and-year format. A link to the archives for previous issues is also in the sidebar. As well, a search box and information about the journal are included here. The main content area lists the table of contents and below that, teaser text for each article. The teasers consist of a title and a set number of characters displayed. Clicking through to an individual article takes you to the post. Social media sharing icons are at the bottom of each article; however, comments are turned off for the website.

Suzanne Sawyer, project coordinator of the National Network of Libraries of Medicine for the MidContinental Region (MCR), answered the survey about her network's usage of WordPress.

The Library and Its Users

The NN/LM covers the MidContinental Region, which consists of six states: Colorado, Kansas, Missouri, Nebraska, Utah, and Wyoming. The headquarters are located at the University of Utah in Salt Lake City. Funding for the organization is provided by the National Library of Medicine.[8] The purpose of the NN/LM is "to provide support to medical libraries and to educate health professionals and the

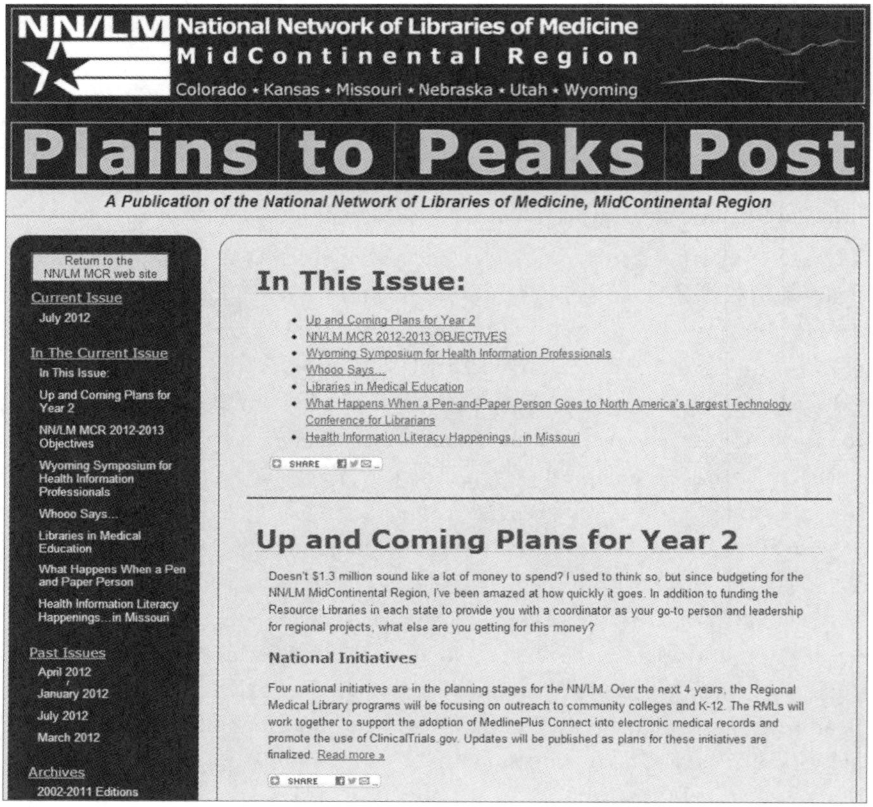

FIGURE 10.2
Plains to Peaks Post site

public about health information," Sawyer writes. Organizations that raise awareness and provide educational resources about health to the public are welcomed to join the NN/LM. These service providers do not necessarily need to be libraries to be eligible for membership.

While the P2PP newsletter is written for medical librarians, the information is not exclusive. Sawyer writes that the primary audience is "health sciences librarians in academic centers and hospitals." However, individuals who have an interest in health also make up the P2PP's targeted audience. For researchers, the journal's archive, which dates back to 2002, is also available online.

Why They Chose WordPress

Before moving to an online format, the P2PP newsletter was a print publication that was mailed to members. However, as with many organizations and publishers, the cost of printing the quarterly newsletter became too great of a burden. It was then decided to distribute the newsletter online. The first attempt was by simply posting PDFs online—a move that Sawyer writes was unpopular among members. Trying to navigate through the articles via PDF was difficult to do, and thus the primary consideration was to make reading the newsletter easier for subscribers.

The decision makers for this online endeavor included Sawyer, the associate director of the NN/LM MCR, and librarians and the staff of the MCR Network. Together they looked at different website options, including Issuu and the Open Journal System (OJS).[9] However, because the NN/LM is a federally funded organization, the Section 508 accessibility standards applied to their online journal. Issuu, being an Adobe Flash–based system, failed to meet the strict accessibility criteria. OJS had an unattractive interface that did not yield an appearance that pleased stakeholders. WordPress was a platform that was popular among other NN/LM regions as it was supported by the national group. Additionally, the organization was already familiar with WordPress—they used it to host a weekly blog. Sawyer writes that "[by] adapting the resources already available to us, I was able to create a template that had the features and appearance that we were looking for in our newsletter."

Building with WordPress

The first stage of building the website was to arrange for server space. This space is hosted on the servers at the University of Washington for the NN/LM. While Sawyer built the site in-house from designing the appearance to coding the site, some outside assistance was provided. Because the NN/LM MCR was being rebranded, a logo for the website was designed at the University of Nebraska by a graphic designer. The appearance of the newsletter was very important to the project. Initially the design was to mimic the original print publication, but it has evolved to better suit the online format since then.

Over the yearlong implementation process, Sawyer worked to modify the WordPress installation to fit the needs of a newsletter. She worked to create a template that was suitable for an online newsletter, implemented features for easier navigation between articles as well as previous issues. The design process took several months. Sawyer writes that the major milestones were "deciding on the platform, creation and approval of the template, testing and debugging, [and then] launching" the site. Site maintenance is done in two ways: plugins are updated as needed, and new content is updated quarterly. As for backing up the site, the University of Washington's web team handles that.

Evaluation

Feedback from NN/LM members has been an important part of the implementation of the online version of the P2PP newsletter. For example, when the PDF system was studied, it was confirmed that navigating and readability of the PDFs was difficult. Members were simply printing out the electronic document. Since moving to the WordPress site, Sawyer writes, "web statistics show that our readership has increased." In the spring of 2013, a questionnaire will be sent out to solicit feedback on this implementation of the newsletter. Sawyer will also ask for ideas on how to improve the website.

Special Features

Sawyer utilizes WordPress's built-in categories, widgets, and custom menus to build the website. First, to create each quarterly issue, she makes a new category titled Month and Year (e.g., April 2012). Then each article for that journal issue is a separate post. Once all the articles have been posted, a final "article" for that issue is created, which is simply a bullet list of all the articles for that quarter. Then in the sidebar, Sawyer adjusts the out-of-the-box Recent Posts widget that comes with WordPress, renamed "In the Current Issue." Sawyer reports that she manually changes the number of posts to show the number of articles in the issue. Thanks to each issue being its own category, she is able to create the "Past Issues" section using the default Categories widget.

Finally, to create the Current Issue link, Sawyer creates a custom menu in WordPress. The menu option on the dashboard is located in the "Appearance" section. To make her menu, Sawyer created a menu titled "Current Issue." Once the Create Menu button is clicked, a new option in the sidebar lets you choose where the custom menu will appear; Sawyer's menu appears in the left sidebar. Next, she adds a link to the current issue's category. This could be done through a custom link, or she could just check off the category for the current issue in the Categories section. Either option works, though using the Categories section is the easier route.

ADDITIONAL LIBRARIES

Mississippi Library Association

www.misslib.com

The MLA packs a lot of information on their website. Aside from numerous helpful links to information about the association itself, the highlight of the website is the job list. Each job post includes all the relevant information about the position. The site's design relies heavily on bullet points.

NOTES

1. Ask a Librarian Delaware Staff, "Ask a Librarian Delaware Provider Libraries," http://aalstaff.lib.de.us/libraries/.

2. Ask a Librarian Delaware Staff, "Contact the Statewide Coordinator," http://aalstaff.lib.de.us/contact/.

3. Ask a Librarian Delaware Staff, "Provider Libraries."

4. Delaware Libraries, http://lib.de.us/.

5. myThemes, "my theme with grass and dew," http://mythem.es/my-world-with-grass-and-dew.

6. internet techies and slidervilla, "Smooth Slider," http://wordpress.org/extend/plugins/smooth-slider/.

7. Michael Torbert, "All in One SEO Pack," http://wordpress.org/extend/plugins/all-in-one-seo-pack/.

8. US National Library of Medicine, www.nlm.nih.gov.

9. Issuu, http://issuu.com/; Open Journal Systems, http://pkp.sfu.ca/?q=ojs.

Chapter Eleven

Digital Libraries/Archives

BETZWOOD

http://mc3betzwood.wordpress.com/

At the Brendlinger Library in Pennsylvania, staff have taken a hyperlocal special collection and shared it with the world at WordPress.com. The library's website celebrates the Betzwood Studios, a turn-of-the-century silent film movie studio located in the county. Materials related to the founder of Betzwood, Siegmund Lubin, are also collected and displayed on the website. Aside from the delightful appearance of the website, the real star is the rich collection of media available to the public. A new feature is the ability to view the films in "HD glory."[1] There are also images, articles, databases, finding aids, and embedded videos throughout the site.

The website is beautiful and designed to invoke the silent-film era, with a yellowed paper background and a film reel edge on the left. The site's header includes an image of the movie studio grounds. The site's official title is listed as "Betzwood: Digital History from the Libraries of Montgomery County Community College." Red accents shine against the background. The bold color is the background for the site's navigation, subtitle, headings, and featured text throughout the website. Therefore the site's strong color contrasts unite the different elements without taking away from the turn-of-the-century artwork that was the silent-film era. As you visit different pages of the website, the site's header has

FIGURE 11.1
Betzwood site

other images superimposed on it to the right featuring Lubin, actors, movie scenes, and more.

On the home page there are two main navigations as seen in the screen shot (fig. 11.1). The first is the red background primary navigation, which runs in a horizontal line across the screen. When text is hovered over, a drop-down menu appears. Then, as you scroll past the introduction, you see a second image-heavy navigation listing again the main navigation. In the footer of the website is the search box.

Interior pages are laid out in two columns. On the left is the main content; the sidebar is to the right. Sidebars may include lists of actors and actresses, timelines, secondary navigation links, or metadata. Comments are turned on for the website, along with social media sharing buttons. A special highlight is using a Google map with colors laid over it to indicate where the studio stood. Areas of interest are identified with pins.

Jerry Yarnetsky, emerging technologies librarian, and Lawrence T. Greene, archives and special collections librarian at the Brendlinger Library of Montgomery County Community College, answered the survey about their library's usage of WordPress.

The Library and Its Patrons

The Brendlinger Library is located in Blue Bell, Pennsylvania, and serves the northwestern suburbs of Philadelphia. The county, which is culturally diverse, has a population of 800,000. While the college had 14,884 students enrolled in the fall of 2011 (according to the college president, Karen Stout), community residents use Brendlinger as a research library.[2] Students range from dual-enrollment high scholars to senior citizens. Technical savviness is not restricted to any one age group, as users on both extremes may be novices or possess advanced skills.

Joseph Eckhardt, the college's history professor, donated his Betzwood collection to the library and archive in early 2012. Eckhardt had spent thirty years researching the studio. During this time, he had given lectures and shared Betzwood's history at the silent film festival. Betzwood produced films from 1912 to 1922 and was the "largest and most technologically advance film studio in the world," Yarnetsky and Greene write. If not for Eckhardt's efforts, the legacy of filmmaking in Montgomery County would have been lost. He realized that the Web provided an opportunity to merge multiple medias together to bring Betzwood's story, films, and cast to a new audience.

When deciding to build an online exhibit, the librarians had two different audiences in mind. First, they wanted a site which would interest and introduce local residents to the county's history. However, they point out that the site's content also needed to "provide articles of sufficient depth to satiate the hungriest film historian." The site's design is therefore fun and engaging, with lots of metadata and links to give researchers more knowledge of the Betzwood film studios.

Why They Chose WordPress

Unlike other libraries surveyed, WordPress was the library's last choice as a platform. The preferred solution was to use Omeka, but the college's technical infrastructure did not support installing a local CMS. So the library reviewed their goals again, write Yarnetsky and Greene:

- to share our collection using industry standards such as OAI-PMH and Dublin Core;
- to use our archive images to tell the stories, not just tell the stories behind individual images;
- to create a custom design that complimented the history we were telling.

Since Omeka was out of the picture, the library reviewed other platforms. It was discovered that no single platform would meet all three goals, so the library decided to pull two platforms together. First, they would host their digital images in the state's CONTENTdm repository. Then the online exhibit would be assembled on WordPress.com. In order to keep the photos with the website, the librarians built custom queries to keep the exhibit together.

Once the library started working with their WordPress.com website, they found the software easy to use and very flexible. Yarnetsky and Greene highlight multiuser authorship, pages, and the ability to customize the theme as attractive features. The website's appearance is an altered version of the Chateau theme.[3] WordPress's built-in flexibility with menus and information architecture has allowed the website to grow in a logical way. Staff was also supported by the technical knowledge of the college's social media team, who also use WordPress.com.

To build such an engaging website requires a collaborative effort. The librarians worked with the library's administration as well as the college's IT and communication departments. The appearance and content were decided upon by Yarnetsky and Greene. After the site had been built, Eckhardt and library staff provided contributions and reviewed the website's content.

Building with WordPress

Before building a digital archive, you need to have content to fill the site before a single line of code can be written for the website. So, Yarnetsky and Greene teamed up with Eckhardt to get the manuscript collection into shape. Greene took over processing the collection and organizing it before digitizing the hundred-year-old silent-film stills. Each item had to be cataloged and then documented in a finding aid. Eckhardt wrote articles and continues to add information as he uncovers more details with his ongoing research. Yarnetsky then built the website. He designed the website and made decisions on how to organize and edit the content to suit their goals.

While the Betzwood collection was formally donated to the library in early 2012, the process to bring the materials to the Web started two years prior. Yarnetsky and Greene note that trying to decide on a platform took a long time. Once WordPress .com was chosen, the site was built (between August 2011 and April 2012). The website's launch coincided with the hundredth anniversary of Betzwood. A grant allowed the library to digitize a dozen films, which then called for a tweaking of the site's design in fall 2012 to integrate the films. Therefore the only new expense for the library was to purchase WordPress's Custom Design upgrade. Otherwise the time intensive process of processing, arranging, describing, and digitizing the collection was done within the library's own budget. Backups of the website are maintained via WordPress.com, which leaves staff to concentrate on the content.

Evaluation

The library has met their goal to introduce local audiences to Betzwood and to provide scholars with invaluable resources. Both communities have responded with an interest to increase the collection and to learn more. Yarnetsky and Greene report that the library has "received several phone calls/e-mails from serious film researchers and descendants of employees/actors regarding use of the materials, both manuscript and video as well as a few researchers informing us that there were items out there in which we might be interested." The site has been successful; in the future, faculty will integrate the collection into their courses.

Aside from direct contact with users, the library reviews WordPress.com's statistics to track their website visitors. Reviewing these statistics has shown that "20% of our traffic is international from 51 nations," according to Yarnetsky and Greene. They express disappointment with the built-in statistics tracker because it does not reveal whether site visitors are local. So the librarians are investigating using a third-party app such as Site Meter to get specific data. The library also tracks how many people come to view the collection in person.[4]

Special Features

The Betzwood site works within the strict limitations of the low-cost Custom Design package. While the entire site is built using only pages, Yarnetsky used clever tricks to bend the Chateau theme to his will. For example, he created custom-coded pages to use as templates in order to add more columns. This effect can be achieved by going into the HTML editor (instead of the Visual editor) and coding a page template by hand. Then this code can be replicated on other pages by copying and pasting it, also using the HTML editor. Yarnetsky added columns and backgrounds by simply adding HTML and CSS to the page. In the style sheet, he would add the extra classes needed to shape the site's appearance. Nonarchival images such as the embedded film backgrounds were uploaded using WordPress's Media Library. Then the links were dropped into the HTML code. The final CSS hack was to remove undesired elements from the theme. While the route on a self-hosted website would be to remove unwanted code from the templates, the Custom Design upgrade gives you access only to the single stylesheet.css file. So when Yarnetsky wanted to remove the date a post was published, he added a line to the style sheet, *display:none*, to hide the post dates. The site's theme is a testimony to the complete ownership of a theme without spending a fortune.

To bring additional media into the website, Yarnetsky relies on embed codes. For example, all the silent films are hosted on YouTube. So Yarnetsky just copies a video's URL, then pastes it into the desired page's body. (If you do this, remember to put the URL on a separate line by itself so the video player will show. Otherwise you will see a plain link in your content.) The other embedded object is the Google map of the former Betzwood location. Yarnetsky and Greene report that "seeing the property over landmarks people recognize today provides a place to the history." This one map furthers Eckhardt's mission to make sure that Betzwood does not fade away. In conjunction with viewing the website, interested visitors can also walk a recreational trail through the area to see some of the surviving structures.

DIGITAL FORSYTH

www.digitalforsyth.org

The Digital Forsyth website is a digital library that promotes the value of the collective memories and artifacts of Forsyth County, North Carolina. What makes this project distinct is the intensive collaborative effort among participating institutions while working within the framework of grant requirements and funding. The goal of the group was to produce a website to strengthen relationships among the institutions while also providing greater service to the community.

Digital Forsyth is a completely customized WordPress installation. Individual artifacts in the collection consist of an image with a caption, the image's metadata, a

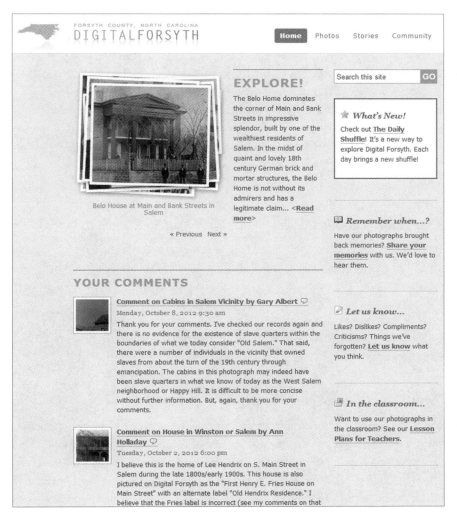

FIGURE 11.2
Digital Forsyth site

comment section, links to similar photos, a print request link, and a box to navigate the site either through filtered keyword searches or by browsing the collection. The website's top navigation includes links to contributed stories and photos, and a link to community, as seen in the screen shot (fig. 11.2). The community section is dedicated to lesson plans for teachers and an invitation to submit photos to the Digital Forsyth Flickr photo group. The twenty-five most recent photos are included on this community page. "Stories" is dedicated to articles about the history of Forsyth County. The right sidebar includes a featured highlight of how to explore Digital Forsyth, links to user involvement, and lesson plans for teachers. User involvement includes a contact form so visitors can submit their memories triggered by the archive's photos, as well as a feedback form. Comments left on individual photos are displayed on the front of the website. The site's overall design is simple with light colors so that the focus remains on the photos and articles.

Kevin Gilbertson, web services librarian at the Z. Smith Reynolds Library at Wake Forest University, answered the survey about his department's usage of WordPress.

The Library and Its Users

Forsyth County is located in central North Carolina. Winston-Salem is the county seat. The county's population was appropriately 355,000 as of 2011.[5] The Digital Forsyth project is a collaborative effort between Wake Forest University's Z. Smith Reynolds Library and Coy C. Carpenter Medical Library, Forsyth County Public Library, Old Salem Museum and Gardens, and Winston-Salem State University's C.G. O'Kelly Library. The combined service population for these groups is difficult to gauge, but is thought to be 230,000 at minimum.[6]

Why They Chose WordPress

In 2004, three Forsyth County libraries met to discuss creating a collaborative project. These joint projects would "increase services for the community" and "increase opportunities for ongoing interlibrary interaction."[6] From this meeting, it was determined that the popular historical photo collections at each institution could be digitized. The mission of the website includes providing access to "cultural, historical, and scientific heritage collections."[7] The effort put forth by the libraries resulted in the August 2007 launch of Digital Forsyth. The project was funded by an Institute of Museum and Library Services (IMLS) grant under the Library Services and Technology Act (LSTA). Decisions about the website were discussed among Wake Forest's User Services team and representatives from each library, according to Gilbertson.

The decision to use WordPress was presented by the Z. Smith Reynolds Library. The library had previous experience in building and customizing WordPress websites. Other platforms were decided against because they "did not provide the level of customization we desired," Gilbertson writes. Furthermore, by using a preexisting and stable platform with a large developer community, staff was free to work on tweaking WordPress for their specific needs instead of starting from scratch.[8]

Building with WordPress

Since the project was funded by a three-year LSTA grant, the website was not implemented until the second year. Gilbertson writes that the first year was spent producing digital content and creating the taxonomy structure. The extensive amount of time working on taxonomy was part of the complete customization efforts done in WordPress. Every step of the project was done in-house among the participating libraries, with Reynolds Library being the technical lead. Many factors were involved: needing a way to handle the Qualified Dublin Core metadata for both importing and display, customizing the user interface, and moving data from another platform to WordPress.[9] The website is hosted and backed up on the Reynolds Library's servers. Since the project is hosted locally, the only new resources purchased were a domain name and additional storage.

119

Browsing is determined by a controlled vocabulary of top-level hierarchy, which is then broken down into subcategories. This browsing capability is what drives the similar photo section on individual item pages. In order to show similar images, the developers "used a Term Frequency/Inverse Document Frequency tag cloud: where normally tag clouds emphasize more popular tags, the Digital Forsyth Similar Photos section inverts it and shows the most similar, aka the least popular," Gilberston writes.

For more in-depth information about Digital Forsyth's complete customization of WordPress, please see the *D-Lib Magazine* article.[10]

Evaluation

Throughout the creation of the website, the project had a user-driven focus that was influenced by results from user surveys and focus groups. The first version of the website was released, and evaluated through additional user testing; then the current website was released. Patron interaction with the website has demonstrated the website to be a valuable resource for their users, Gilbertson reports. Users have indicated they continue to be delighted by the website as the photos stir up forgotten memories. Additionally, the libraries received online feedback through the website's contact forms. Gary Albert, the editorial director at the Old Salem

Museums & Gardens, reports that requests for copies of their high-resolution photos has gone up 155 percent. At the time of the survey for this book, no new content or assessments were being done because the three-year term of the grant had ended.

Special Features

Since Digital Forsyth was developed intensely beyond a standard WordPress installation, there are no public plugins available. The web developers created the search box, metadata, and image viewer, Gilbertson writes. Details about how the team crafted many of these elements can be found in their published article.[11]

Each individual artifact on the website is represented by a single blog post. The articles on the website were written by people hired via grant funding; these writers may be local residents or researchers. Together the efforts of these people populated the content of the website. For your own website, you can use the help of local residents to gather data about your digital collections. Often, older people may volunteer to describe and research photographic collections. If they are lifelong residents, they may be able to identify buildings and landmarks that have since disappeared. A helpful tool for these volunteers would be a complete set of phone books so that buildings identified in photos can be located at a physical address. With this information in hand, your library could then build a Google map superimposed over current satellite data.[12]

MADISON LIBRARY LOCAL HISTORY

www.madisonlibrary-nh.org/madisonhistory/

Community archives consist of materials that are of local historical significance. Prairienet discusses how community archives are used to represent underserved populations and serve as the collective memory of the community.[13] Materials may already be within the library's collection in the case of academic libraries or the library may actively solicit the community for new items. Digital archives produced by academic libraries often rely on expensive software such as CONTENTdm.[14] However, as the Madison Library Local History Project proves, you can build an attractive and useful community archive when there is not a budget for specialized archival software by using WordPress.

While faced with limited resources but a rich local history collection, the Madison Library Local History Project was built in house as a community digital

Madison Library
Local History Project
A community digital archive for Madison, New Hampshire

| Home | Just added | Books, pamphlets, letters | Maps | Photos, images | Vital stats, obituaries | Oral histories |

About

The Madison Library's Local History Project is a community endeavor coordinated by the library, and compiled by volunteers. We are just getting started, and we could use more volunteers. Contact Mary Cronin at the library if you're interested. Training is provided.

Here is some of what we are working on now:

- Scanning historical items in the library's collection. These include Old Home Week booklets, postcards of Madison, Madison High School Yearbooks.
- Indexing old newspaper clippings, mostly obituaries.
- Indexing vital records.
- Transcribing manuscripts.

Here is what we would like to get started:

- Collecting oral histories from people in town. We will provide a digital recorder, an interview guide, an recording log, and a release form.

Contact Mary Cronin at the Madison Library if you'd like to help or find out more, 603-367-8545 or librarian@madison.lib.nh.us.

Madison, NH info

- Madison Library
- Town of Madison

Other sites with Madison history

Search Site [Q]

Supporters

- Moose Plate Conservation Grant
- The Pequawket Foundation

Contribute!

Do you have an item of local historical interest that would be suitable for this archive? If you do or think you do, please contact us. We can make facsimile copies if you would like to keep your original.

Browse by date

- Up to 1852
- 1852-1859
- 1860-1869
- 1870-1879
- 1880-1889
- 1890-1899
- 1900-1909
- 1910-1919
- 1920-1929
- 1930-1939
- 1940-1949
- 1950-1959
- 1960-1969
- 1970-1979

121

FIGURE 11.3
Madison Library Local History site

archive. The project consists of high-quality images, downloadable yearbooks, oral history transcripts, and local written materials. Each record item has metadata attached to its entry. WordPress's native category and tagging system is used for the site's information architecture, as can be seen in the screen shot (fig. 11.3). Access to the collection is through top-level categories based on material type. The items can also be browsed by decade or descriptive tags. Nonimage files can be viewed via links to the resource. The archive's strengths lie in its clear navigation and easy access to the materials.

Mary Cronin, director of the Madison Library located in Madison, New Hampshire, answered the survey about her library's usage of WordPress.

The Library and Its Users

The Madison Library is a rural public library located on the eastern side of New Hampshire. The library has a service population of 2,500 people. While patrons have access to broadband, many prefer to use their mobile devices. Popular mobile activities include accessing e-mail and using social media. As far as technical skills, the patrons have a range of abilities and interest from the early adopters to those who have yet to use a computer. In Cronin's assessment, the diversity of technical knowledge is spread throughout the population. The residents voiced support when the library discussed displaying their local history online. As well, the library trustees and historical society also backed the archive initiative.

Why They Chose WordPress

The purpose of the Madison Library Local History Project was to create an accessible site that could display Madison's unique historical items. After receiving a Moose Plate Conservation Grant in 2007, a specialist from the Northeast Document Conversation Center visited the Madison Library. While looking through the library's vault, Cronin writes, staff realized "that Madison's 20th century history was not being collected in any organized way, but was quickly being lost as longtime residents passed away and their heirs cleaned out houses and barns that had been in the same family for generations." The library held public meetings to gain support for the initiative.

Cronin viewed other New Hampshire archives such as Beyond Brown Paper, another WordPress website, for guidance and inspiration.[15] WordPress's intuitive interface and Cronin's previous experience in building the library's website in WordPress were the reasons she chose it as her CMS over Joomla and Omeka. Cronin's educational background in using WordPress was developed through attending a state library workshop on WordPress led by Bobbi Slosser, the NH State Library's technology resources librarian. Slosser and the NH WordPress Users Google Group have offered Cronin support in overcoming technical challenges.

Building with WordPress

The library had wanted to create an online archive for years but lacked the staff and funding to do so. Therefore, once the project was approved by stakeholders, Cronin built the website by working unpaid hours on the weekends and in the evenings. Cronin's background in graphic and book design helped her design the attractive website. The project is hosted on a subdomain of the library's website; the WordPress software is installed on the library's own server.

The launch of the project marked the end of a two year process to build a website from the time it was decided that a website best met the library's needs. The first major milestone of the project was obtaining a grant to purchase ABBYY Finereader software, an optical character recognition program. This software allows text in PDFs to be searched, which assists the accessibility of the document as a whole. Cronin notes that ABBYY Finereader can even read "some of the unusual typefaces found in 100-year old booklets." The next milestone was launching the website in the summer of 2012. Before going live with the site, Cronin spent months experimenting with different content management platforms, themes, and plugins, and setting up the navigational scheme. (Slosser gave Cronin the idea to make the content browsable by decade.)

Site maintenance is done by Cronin. Content is digitized by three volunteers, who submit it to Cronin to be uploaded to the website. Backups of the website and digital files are saved onto two large 2 terabyte (TB) hard drives. The hard drives were obtained through a local history grant.

Evaluation

Since the project launched just two months before the time of this writing, there is no historical data on the website usage. However, Cronin notes that "the site is [already] meeting the goals of providing better access to Madison's local history." She expects that promotion of the website will be done primarily through word of mouth—especially in such a small town! The volunteers have been enthusiastic supporters, with one of the ladies in particular spreading word about the website and her contributions to it.

Site traffic is being examined through the use of Google Analytics. Cronin is interested in finding out how people are finding the project (i.e., where site traffic originates from) and which pages get the most views. By looking at the popularity of the pages, she is able to judge which items are of the most interest. In the future, she plans to do a user survey or feedback session to gain insight on what features need to be improved.

Special Features

The standout features for this website include the high-quality images, metadata, navigation, and searchable transcripts of scanned files. First, the yearbook files are scanned in at an archival quality of 600 dpi, making them too large to be uploaded through WordPress's Media Library. Thus the yearbooks are uploaded to Cronin's own server, and links to the files are provided on the yearbook's entry on the website. While these files are very large, the ability to link to files easily within WordPress makes it easy in turn to keep materials connected to one another.

Next, Cronin admired how Omeka detects, collects, and displays uploaded file data (e.g. file size) automatically. Therefore, for the project, each object's metadata description fields are a simplified form of Dublin Core, which is entered manually.[16] The current fields in use include information from the file type, a link to the field, a physical item description, and any identifying information, such as a title page. This information is entered into each post's body text box. Eventually, Cronin would like "to develop a simplified version of Omeka's upload form in WordPress so that people can add their own items to our site and provide the descriptive elements we need to fit the navigation scheme and to add searchability."

Cronin makes clever use of WordPress default categories and tags, allowing for further discoverability by material type, decade of creation, and subject. In WordPress's category settings, she set up a category for each material type and decade pairing. When she adds a new object, she then selects a category to identify the material type and date created. In the tag field, keyword terms, such as a person's name, are added to better describe the item.

Finally, the original handwritten news columns of Alice Ward have provided an in-depth look into Madison's history. However, the paper's fragility has rendered that unsuitable as accessible materials. Instead the library's volunteers have transcribed the columns. The ABBYY Finereader software makes the transcripts searchable for residents seeking information about relatives.

ADDITIONAL LIBRARIES

A Compendium of Digital Collections

http://digitalcollections.wordpress.com/

The Compendium is no longer active. However, the website is still available online as a valuable resource to foster communication between librarians and researchers. Each post lists a different digital research that may be of interest to researchers which they may not have heard of otherwise.

Engineering Studies Student Research Archive

http://sites.lafayette.edu/esarchive/

This digital repository is not a library website or project. However, the students did consult with library staff to determine the best platform to achieve their goals. This repository displays uploaded projects from the students. Each project is one post that includes metadata about the topic and includes tags.

The Henselt Library at European-American University

http://henseltlibrary.wordpress.com/

While many digital libraries and archives must be very concerned with copyright, the Henselt Library gives access to rare public domain piano scores from the nineteenth century. Each score is presented as a PDF for easy downloading and printing. The site's navigation is through tabbed pages across the top. Each page consists of links to PDFs for a section of letters of the alphabet (e.g., A–D, E–H).

125

History of Missiology

http://digilib.bu.edu/mission/

This digital library/archive is a joint project of the Boston University Theology Library and the Center for Global Christianity and Mission. A highlight of the website is the biography index. Each biography includes the person's photo, a brief overview of their mission work, and a bibliography of additional resources for that person.

Langworthy Public Library

http://langworthylibrary.org/

The library's archives are uploaded to their WordPress website using a plugin. To help arrange your photos to a similar effect, you can use the WP Photo Album Plus plugin.[17] Additionally, the library has videos of their oral history Depot Square Interviews.

Salisbury NH History

http://history.salisburynh.net/

This small digital archive website uses a slideshow to great effect. The website is dominated by large images. Some letters in the archive has been transcribed, while others are scans displayed in galleries.

Special Collections and University Archives at Umass Amherst Libraries

www.library.umass.edu/spcoll/umarmot/

This beautiful, tightly woven website features an interactive "catablog" of special materials. Collections can be browsed by letter, category, department, keyword, or project. Digital projects link to individual project websites.

NOTES

1. "Betzwood: Libraries of Montgomery County Community College," http://mc3betzwood.wordpress.com/.

2. Linda Stein, "Growing Pains at Montgomery Community College," 2012, http://mainlinemedianews.com/articles/2012/04/27/king_of_prussia_courier/news/doc4f9a170846493062837131.txt.

3. Ignacio Ricci, "Chateau," http://theme.wordpress.com/themes/chateau/.

4. "Site Meter," www.sitemeter.com/.

5. United States Census Bureau, "State & County QuickFacts: Forsyth County, North Carolina," http://quickfacts.census.gov/qfd/states/37/37067.html.

6. Krishna Brown, Amanda Goodman, Stephanie Jobe, and Rebecca Petersen, "Needs Assessment of Coy C. Carpenter Library," assignment, University of North Carolina Libraries of Montgomery County Community College, http://mc3betzwood.wordpress.com/.

7. Linda Stein, "Growing Pains at Greensboro, 2010"; Forsyth County Public Library, "Library Statistics," www.forsyth.cc/library/statistics.aspx; Winston-Salem State University, "Collection Development," www.wssu.edu/cg-okelly-library/departments/collection-development.aspx.

8. Elizabeth Skinner, Carter Cue, and Susan Smith, "Digital Forsyth: An NCECHO Collaborative Multli-year Digitization Project," 2007, www.slideshare.net/smithss_27106/ncla-df-wfu.

9. Digital Forsyth, "Mission and Vision," www.digitalforsyth.org/about/mission-vision.php.

10. Erik Mitchell and Kevin Gilbertson, "Using Open Source Social Software as Digital Library Interface," *D-Lib Magazine* Volume 14 Number ¾ (2008), www.dlib.org/dlib/march08/mitchell/03mitchell.html.

11. Ibid.

12. "Google Map Maker," https://www.google.com/mapmaker.

13. Prairienet, "Community Archives Approach," 2011, www.prairienet.org/op/digarch/approaches-for-smaller-community-institutions/community-archiving/.

14. OCLC, "CONTENTdm," www.contentdm.org.

15. Beyond Brown Paper, http://beyondbrownpaper.plymouth.edu/.

16. Dublin Core Metadata Initiative, "Semantic Recommendations," http://dublincore.org/specifications/.

17. opajaap, "WP Photo Album Plus," http://wordpress.org/extend/plugins/wp-photo-album-plus/.

Chapter Twelve

Government and Law

ENERGY, ECONOMICS AND THE ENVIRONMENT

http://supplements.kentlaw.iit.edu/energylawcasebook

E-books are currently one of the most pressing concerns right now in libraries. Studies have been predicting for years that the rise of electronic textbooks will replace physical textbooks while other studies proclaim that students will never adapt. At the Illinois Institute of Technology (IIT)'s Chicago-Kent College of Law Library, they have decided to jump right into the foray by creating an online component to a traditional textbook using WordPress: The Energy, Economics and the Environment: A Casebook Supplement Site. The website was created at the request of a faculty member. Each month new articles are added, which keeps the site from becoming outdated.

When first encountering the supplement website, there appears to be no indicator that this site is powered by WordPress. The only giveaway is at the bottom of the page, where the theme's designer, NattyWP, is listed along with a tiny WordPress logo. Otherwise the site has a top bar which lists ways to subscribe to the website and a search box. The site's title and purpose is laid out below this top bar, as seen in the screen shot (fig. 12.1). The site's front page includes a photo of the physical textbook, links to the authors' websites, a listing of recent posts, and the book's publication information. Below this information is the table of contents, which makes it easy to jump down to the relevant chapter. A link to each major section within a chapter goes to a list of related posts. Some of the sections that have a link may have no posts; if there are posts for a chapter, the summary includes a

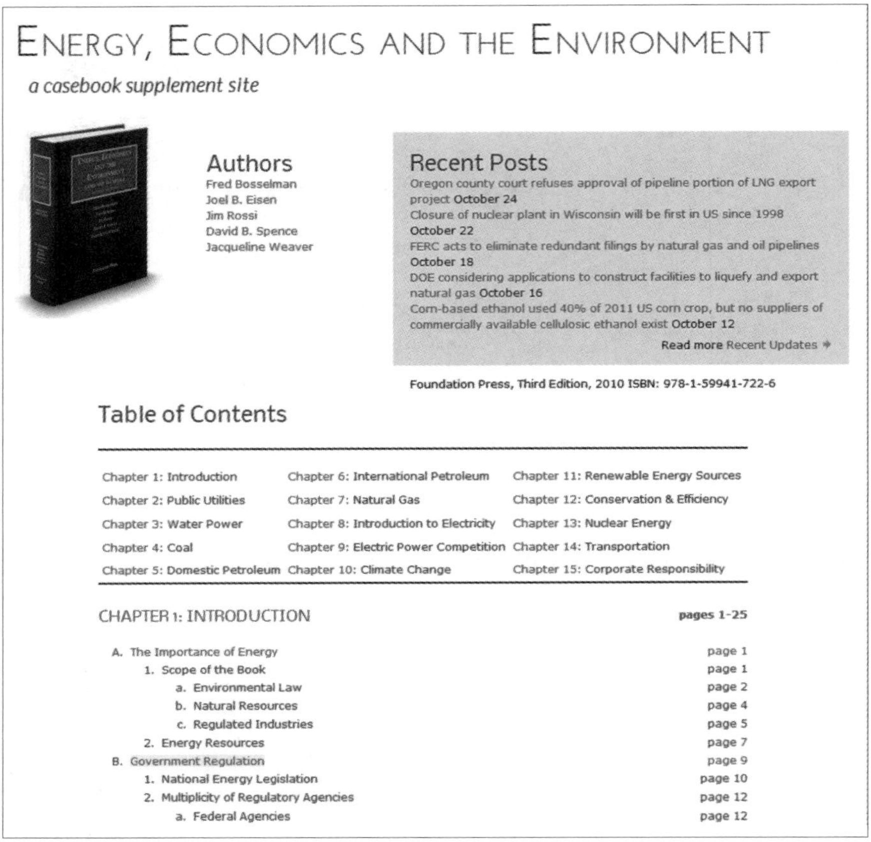
ENERGY, ECONOMICS AND THE ENVIRONMENT
a casebook supplement site
Authors
Fred Bosselman
Joel B. Eisen
Jim Rossi
David B. Spence
Jacqueline Weaver
Recent Posts
Oregon county court refuses approval of pipeline portion of LNG export project October 24
Closure of nuclear plant in Wisconsin will be first in US since 1998 October 22
FERC acts to eliminate redundant filings by natural gas and oil pipelines October 18
DOE considering applications to construct facilities to liquefy and export natural gas October 16
Corn-based ethanol used 40% of 2011 US corn crop, but no suppliers of commercially available cellulosic ethanol exist October 12
Read more Recent Updates
Foundation Press, Third Edition, 2010 ISBN: 978-1-59941-722-6
Table of Contents
Chapter 1: Introduction
Chapter 2: Public Utilities
Chapter 3: Water Power
Chapter 4: Coal
Chapter 5: Domestic Petroleum
Chapter 6: International Petroleum
Chapter 7: Natural Gas
Chapter 8: Introduction to Electricity
Chapter 9: Electric Power Competition
Chapter 10: Climate Change
Chapter 11: Renewable Energy Sources
Chapter 12: Conservation & Efficiency
Chapter 13: Nuclear Energy
Chapter 14: Transportation
Chapter 15: Corporate Responsibility
CHAPTER 1: INTRODUCTION
pages 1-25
A. The Importance of Energy page 1
1. Scope of the Book page 1
a. Environmental Law page 2
b. Natural Resources page 4
c. Regulated Industries page 5
2. Energy Resources page 7
B. Government Regulation page 9
1. National Energy Legislation page 10
2. Multiplicity of Regulatory Agencies page 12
a. Federal Agencies page 12

FIGURE 12.1
Energy, Economics, and the Environment site

photo, a title, the section the post is listed under, a text excerpt from the post, and a horizontal list of tags. Each post may have a comment from an author of the book, but all posts have a quote from an additional resource. The source information for the quote is then listed. Comments are sometimes turned on for a post. On these individual pages, the right sidebar contains the book's photo and list of authors. There is also a widget displaying the latest posts. The archives are organized by chapter, with links to subscription services per chapter by RSS or via e-mail. The archive can also be searched by month.

Emily Barney, library web technologist at the IIT Chicago-Kent College of Law in Chicago, answered the survey about her library's usage of WordPress.

The Library and Its Users

The Library at IIT Chicago-Kent College of Law is located in downtown Chicago, just west of Lake Michigan. The fall 2011 population of full-time and part-time students was 944 people.[1] Students who attend the school are studying to be lawyers. Additionally, students may be entering the field of intellectual property rights.[2] Barney writes that students have a wide range of technical knowledge from those who "avoid technology if possible [...] or [want me] to take on maintenance myself to advanced users who just need me to get them started and hand over the keys." Access to the Internet is not restricted by location.

Why They Chose WordPress

A faculty member of the college was publishing a book in 2010. He approached the library to discuss creating an always-current supplemental website for his book. His concern was that "this book will be out of date as soon as it is published," Barney writes. He also requested a solution that would be easy to update and would integrate well with his book. Staff, who had previous experience with WordPress, realized that the platform's hierarchical category system would be easy to configure to match the book's table of contents, and so they suggested WordPress. After showing the professor the back end of a WordPress installation, he agreed with their assessment.

With the professor's blessing, library staff needed to then obtain permission to create the website. First, they contacted the publishers and the coauthors for their permission. With their approval, the library then contacted the dean of the school. The dean allotted funding to hire a student to handle post creation for the website's first year. It was then time to build the website.

Building with WordPress

In the early days, the library hosted the supplemental website on their own servers. The site's domain was provided by the law school's IT staff. For the site's theme, a basic one was used; after the site moved to the live server, the professor specified the site's appearance from there. Thanks to the library's previous experience, the site was entirely built in-house. Once the site's structure and appearance were settled, it was time to pull in the content that the professor had set aside for the website. The hired student worked on the post creation. Once most of the content was up, the site was then promoted to students. When the paid year was up, the responsibility of posting was transferred over to the library. Each month the professor sends his additions via e-mail to staff for upload. Since the site's launch, the professor has semiretired, so postings have reduced.

The website's future is unknown at this point due to the retirement of the faculty member. Barney and the library "expect [the website] may shift to the control of the other authors in the next year." If this happens, the library may transfer the site over to a coauthor's institution or may continue to host it. As for the site's design, the library hopes to move their custom code to a child theme for a basic framework.

Since launch, the site has been moved to a new server and was given a new URL to correspond with changes to the law school website, Barney reports. Before any new features are added, the changes are tested on the development site. By taking these precautions, the library has not run into any major site issues as WordPress continues to develop.

Evaluation

The site continues to please the professor. Site statistics are monitored through the Jetpack plugin.[3] Another professor at the college has expressed interest in using a similar setup to create a supplement site for her published book. With such requests in mind, the library hopes to "build out into similar sites at other institutions," Barney writes. The library has given presentations about their work at Harvard and at the 2011 Computer Assisted Legal Instruction conference. The slides and a video of the presentation can be viewed online.[4] Overall, Barney notes that the experience has taught the library that while the project has been enjoyable, "it requires a great deal of content and constant attention to the subject matter to create an entire site of supplementary materials for a book."

Special Features

As mentioned previously, the website uses WordPress categories and the Jetpack plugin. Each major chapter is a parent category; each section within that parent chapter is a child category. The simplicity of organizing posts this way to match the book's table of content made the site easy for the hired student to use. (A screenshot of a post view can be seen on slide ten of Barney's slide presentation.[5]) With the posts assigned to the correct categories, the site's front page is "hard-coded to the categories and styled with CSS," Barney writes. The term *hard-coded* means that instead of harnessing the dynamic category display of a CMS, each link in the table of contents is manually typed onto the front page (usually on an index.php file). In the future, the library would like to use dynamic categories but have not placed this function on the website.

Barney mentions that the Jetpack plugin is only being used to monitor their website's statistics. However, the plugin is advertised as "supercharg[ing] your self-hosted WordPress website with the awesome cloud power of WordPress.com."[6] A few of the highlights for this plugin include e-mail subscriptions for posts, full-screen photo galleries, social sharing links, and a way to display mathematical expressions. These and other features of Jetpack are not baked into the default WordPress installation, so the website's developer can decide exactly how they want their website to function.

THE STATE LAW LIBRARY OF MONTANA

http://mtlawlibrary.wordpress.com/

The ability to assess information and recognize bias is an important part of information literacy. The Association of College and Research Libraries (ACRL) includes this bias-detecting skill in their "Information Literacy Competency Standards for Higher Education." The standard states that "the information literate student articulates and applies initial criteria for evaluating both the information and its sources."[7] The State Law Library of Montana provides information only about the Supreme Court opinions and orders. This information is provided without commentary and gives no space for discussion. Thus, users of the legal documents can seek accurate information without encountering personal opinions.

The website is hosted for free on WordPress.com. The tagline clearly states the purpose of the website: "Notices of new Opinions and Orders from the Montana Supreme Court, Library Announcements, Research Tips, and Montana Legal News." Site navigation is in a horizontal menu on the website. Layout of the site is in three columns, as seen in the screen shot (fig. 12.2). On the left is a calendar (with dates in bold if the website was updated that day), links to oral arguments, archives, and meta information for the site administrator. In the center column are summaries of the latest posts. These postings are in reverse chronological order, in a traditional blog format. In the right column is a link to subscribe to the website via e-mail, a tag cloud of frequent topics, a keyword search box, and the website's category listings. Individual posts include footer navigational links to posts before and after the current post.

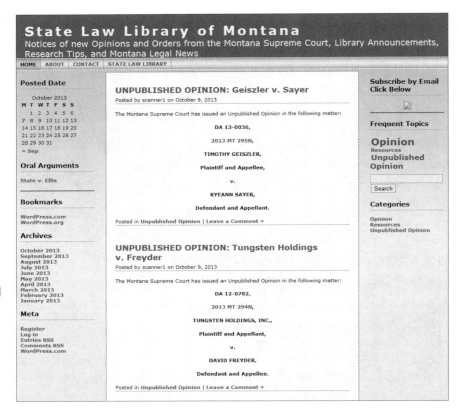

FIGURE 12.2
State Law Library of Montana site

Judy Meadows, director and state law librarian at the State Law Library of Montana, answered the survey about her library's usage of WordPress.

The Library and Its Users

The State Law Library of Montana is located in Helena, Montana. Helena is located west of the center of the state. The estimated population of Montana in 2011 was just over 998,000.[8] Therefore the library is serving a small population dispersed across a very large state. Meadows writes that "we rely on mobile access, which is prevalent." Since mobile access is widespread here, the patrons are very technologically literate. This reliance on mobility means that the library's resources need to be easy to access for users on the go. The goal then of the library is to be a patron's first stop for "good, authentication information," Meadows writes, rather than bad search engine results.

Why They Chose WordPress

As the state's only public law library, there is not a lot of time for learning complicated website platforms or programs. So the library needed a platform that would be quick to learn and easy to use and maintain. However, the ultimate advantage to WordPress was being able "to present the information the way we want," Meadows writes. This aspect is important when dealing with potentially highly polarized legal opinions.

Building with WordPress

The original website for the library was built in 1994. Since that time, the website has undergone a redesign every three to five years. The WordPress website was put together in-house, but the current implementation was designed by an outside web designer. The content is managed by staff who load, change, edit, and move posts as needed. The state government's IT handles the site's maintenance and backup.

Evaluation

The library solicits feedback on the site continuously. In particular, the users who are asked to test the website are the lower courts, public libraries, attorneys, and clerks of court, Meadows writes. Information about how users navigate the site provides additional discoveries about how users navigate the website.

"Our customers love our website, and we know from our statistics that it is one of the most heavily used of all Montana state government websites," Meadows reports.

Special Features

For the State Law Library of Montana, social features and comments are not features that their website needs. By moving away from these Web 2.0 attributes, the website stands as a testimony to legal rulings without the fiery debates that erupt on many newspaper websites. To turn off the comments on a WordPress website, go to the Settings menu, then click on the Discussion link. At the top of the page, in the Default article settings, uncheck the Allow People to Post Comments on New

Articles box. (By default, WordPress always enables comments on every installation, even for self-hosted sites.)

If your site is older and you decide to remove the ability for readers to comment, you will need to follow a different procedure. Your first option is to visit each post and page individually and uncheck the comment box below the body box. An easier option is to bulk-disable comments. First, go to your All Posts or All Pages menu link. Then click the checkbox next to the word Title in the upper left listing of your posts or pages. Then click on the Bulk Actions drop down menu above this checkbox to select Edit. Click the Apply button. A new Bulk Edit menu will appear. Look for the word Comments on the right side of the menu. Click on No Change and then select Do Not Allow. Finish up by hitting Update; check your website to make sure all the comment boxes have disappeared.

Another possibility is that you may have a theme that refuses to obey your objective to remove comments completely. In this case, you need to edit the theme. (A word of caution: whenever you edit the theme, make sure you have a backup copy before you start just in case disaster strikes.) There are a variety of ways to access and edit your theme's files. You can work within WordPress's native theme editor, or you can FTP to your site's server and pull the php templates from there into your preferred code editor. If you use WordPress's built-in access to the template files, you may want to copy the text from each template, paste it into a code editor, and run a find operation to remove the text. Then you would carefully copy the entire page and paste it back into the WordPress templates through the theme editor.

To access the theme files through your self-hosted WordPress website, go the Appearance menu and then click on Editor. What you want to do is delete lines of PHP that say *comments_template*. You may also need to delete other lines that include the word *comment* in them. You will likely need to remove these <? Php *comments_template;* ?> lines from more than one PHP theme file (and they may not look exactly like that!). The usual suspects are blog.php, page.php, home .php, index.php, and single.php (as in a single post) files. If your theme is very complicated, you may have more than a dozen PHP theme files to edit. Just take your time to make backups before you start.

ADDITIONAL LIBRARIES

Library of Congress Blog

http://blogs.loc.gov/loc/

WordPress has been used for years by the Library of Congress for their collection blog. Posts are organized by category, and content can be found through a keyword search. The library's latest tweet is displayed in the sidebar and uses the Flexo Archives plugin to control the display of the blog's archives.[9]

Oral History in the Digital Age

http://ohda.matrix.msu.edu/

A collaborative effort among a number of library institutions and museums, the Oral History site is a how-to guide for working with oral histories. The site's theme is Graphene, which uses drop-down menus.[10] Posts are organized by tag and category in the right sidebar.

ReferencePoint

http://referencepoint.apps.gov/

New posts to this blog ended after July 31, 2012. The site was produced by the US National Library of Medicine. The site's purpose was to provide a list of medical references aimed at other librarians. An interesting aspect of the website was a list in the sidebar displaying how many times various posts had been viewed. Posts could be given a star rating using the WP-PostRatings plugin.[11]

Suggestion Box at IIT Downtown Campus Library

http://library.kentlaw.iit.edu/blogs/suggestions/

Feedback from students is important at this law library. Students submit an online form, which is then sorted into a variety of categories: complaints, kudos, questions, reporting problems, and suggestions. Comments are then publically answered by the library. The comment form is the popular Contact Form 7 plugin.[12]

NOTES

1. IIT Chicago-Kent College of Law, "Student Body Profile," www.kentlaw.iit.edu/prospective-students/jd-program-admissions/student-body-profile.

2. IIT Chicago-Kent College of Law, "Master of IP Management & Markets," www.kentlaw.iit.edu/academics/master-of-ip-management-and-markets.

3. automattic et al., "Jetpack by WordPress.com," http://wordpress.org/extend/plugins/jetpack/.

4. Emily Barney, "Marketing Faculty Expertise: Casebook Supplement Sites," 2011, www.slideshare.net/EBarney/casebook-supplements-slides; Barney, "Casebooks Unbound: Online Supplements with WordPress," YouTube video, 1:00:06, posted by "caliorg," July 14, 2011, www.youtube.com/watch?v=-qxorR_xDdI.

5. Ibid., "Markteing Faculty Expertise."

6. automatic et al., "Jetpack."

7. Association of College & Research Libraries, "Information Literacy Competency Standards for Higher Education," www.ala.org/acrl/standards/informationliteracycompetency.

8. United States Census Bureau, "State & Country QuickFacts: Montana," http://quickfacts.census.gov/qfd/states/30000.html.

9. Heath Harrelson, "Flexo Archives," http://wordpress.org/extend/plugins/flexo-archives-widget/.

10. silverks, "Graphene," http://wordpress.org/extend/themes/graphene.

11. Lester Chan, "WP-PostRatings," http://wordpress.org/extend/plugins/wp-postratings/.

12. takayukister, "Contact Form 7," http://wordpress.org/extend/plugins/contact-form-7/.

Chapter Thirteen

Public Libraries

THE GROVE LIBRARY

http://thegrovelibrary.net/

The Grove Library website is a beautiful, seemingly simple website with a great user interface. The needs of the online patron have been thought through thoroughly. For instance, the navigation uses simple, direct language such as "Find" and "Services For," which eliminates some of the uncertainties of where to click to find information. By hovering over one of the top horizontal menus, a drop-down menu appears, which also responds to natural questions a user may ask. Examples include: "What you can borrow or browse," "How to join," and "See what I have out." This kind of forwardness is an illustration of best practices from Steve Krug's book, *Don't Make Me Think: A Common Sense Approach to Web Usability*.[1] This bestselling usability book boils down to this: remove any obstacles that make your user pause to think what that image/word/navigational element means. One of his best examples is that *job* is a more user-friendly word than *career* or *employment*. Be short, simple, and direct. The Grove Library website exemplifies this philosophy.

Simplicity, as we have seen above, rules this library's website. The clean theme is Suffusion by Sayontan Sinha.[2] Branding in the site's header dominates the eye immediately, with the orange standing out in sharp relief to the white and gray of the rest of the site. The main navigation looks like tabs, which reveal drop-down menus when hovered over. Below is a second row of navigation in the form of buttons for the user's account, the library's catalog, hours, and a contact us link.

FIGURE 13.1
The Grove Library site

Beside these buttons is a search box, as seen in the screen shot (fig. 13.1). The website's home page shows main content in the form of posts on the left and a single column on the right. The column includes a newsletter subscription link, newsletter archive, a link to the events calendar, a button to the local history images, featured events, social media buttons, a widget displaying how to get a library card, and finally a virtual tour video. The website's footer is the library's logo written in a large font. Comments are turned on for posts. The site's other distinguishing feature is the number of outside platforms that are neatly integrated into the website. For example, the library's catalog is displayed within the same framework as the rest of the website, so you have the library's header, navigation, and footer surrounding the vendor's embedded catalog. By keeping the library's website around most of the outside content, the user never has the impression that they are leaving the main website at any point and thus have a unified experience.

Kathryn Greenhill, associate lecturer in Information Studies at Curtin University in Perth, Western Australia, answered the survey about her library's usage of WordPress. She was formerly the special services librarian at the Grove Library in Perth.[3]

The Library and Its Users

Perth is the capitol of the state of Western Australia, located on the southwest cost of the continent. The population of Perth is 1.74 million people as of June 2011.[4] The Grove was created and funded by three government areas: the Town of Cottesloe, the Shire of Peppermint Grove, and the Town of Mosman Park.[5] Nestled amongst these three areas, the Grove Library is located in an affluent suburb of Perth between the Indian Ocean and the broad Swan River. Thus the majority of patrons are "older, well-educated and from a European background," Greenhill writes. She also notes that the library's members tend to be young families, teens, tourists, the elderly, and some business users. The surrounding neighborhood includes a few public housing residents. Users are more likely to use a Mac for their web browsing than the general population.

Why They Chose WordPress

In July 2010, the new Grove Library opened after the three aforementioned government areas came together to build a library. A major change included renaming the library, it's the former Cottesloe/Peppermint Grove/Mosman Park Library. With the new imaginative, inviting name of the Grove, it was also decided to rebrand the library's online presence with a new website. The previous website had been hosted on the server of a marketing firm. To make any changes to this website, such as adding multimedia or an RSS feed, was very expensive.

The library was fortunate to have Greenhill, who was already an expert in WordPress. She was able to build the website in-house and make all the customizations the library needed. As well, Greenhill was supported by her colleague who shared the job of special services librarian with her. The colleague learned WordPress as well. The funding for this new website venture came from the city librarian's budget.

141

At the beginning, WordPress was meant to be a "'stopgap' measure before transferring the library website to Drupal a year after the new building opened," Greenhill states. It was then realized that the vast support community, the variety of customization offers available through themes and plugins, and the flexibility of WordPress were all an ideal fit for the Grove Library. At year's end, it was decided that the library would stay with the platform.

Building with WordPress

Greenhill set to work on designing and developing the new website. First, server space had to be purchased from Bluehost. Then, Greenhill reports, the library purchased multiple domain URLs in order to prevent "typo squatters" from trying to edge in on the library's turf. (A nonlibrary example of "typo squatting" is that Blockbuster purchased the domain of *netlix.com* so that when someone mistypes *netflix.com* the user is redirected to Blockbuster's website. Blockbuster and Netflix are business rivals). The library considered hiring their marketing company to create a new WordPress theme before realizing this was beyond the agency's capabilities. Instead, the library requested "a style guide that included colours, fonts and provided us with a number of standardised brand-based images that we could use in the header-banner throughout the site," Greenhill writes. The library then placed these agency created images within the website's Suffusion theme. (More information about the decision to use the Suffusion can be found on Greenhill's blog.[6])

The site's architecture is built using pages and posts. Pages are for long-term information, such as "About the Library" and "What Are Member Benefits." The posts are time sensitive and list upcoming events and happenings. In the sidebar, each section is made up of different widgets. Some widgets are just clickable images, while another is a list of featured posts using categories.

The timeline for the new website's development was four months. The major milestones involved creating a test website and deciding on the website's information architecture. Once the site's structure was in place, the library launched the new website using the old site's branding elements. This strategy was used to give patrons a continuous experience as their community library evolved from the old to the new. The members could access their library's new website a month before the new library building opened. To mark the transition, Greenhill switched out the old site design elements for the new one—and thus the Grove Library website was born!

Evaluation

Since Greenhill has left the Grove, Jonathan Gurney, the e-services librarian, answered questions about how the new site continues to meet the library's needs. He reports that the revamped website has been successful. Using Google Analytics, the library saw more than 93,000 visits between November 2010 and November 2012. Users are spending 2.25 minutes on the site on average. The Grove has also responded to user feedback, such as adding a drop-down menu for digital subscription services, event registration forms, and a widget for users to sign up for a newsletter. These subsequent adjustments have continued to provide a great user experience for site visitors, Gurney reports.

Special Features

The forms on the Grove Library website are done using the cforms plugin.[7] (Please note that this plugin is not available from the WordPress plugin repository because the plugin does not adhere to WordPress's open source license.) Greenhill writes that cforms creates more customizable forms than other plugins. Examples of how other websites have customized their forms can be found on the plugin's website by clicking on the Random User Examples link. The Grove uses cforms for the membership registration, general inquiries, interlibrary loan, and the library's "homebound" delivery services forms, Greenhill notes.

Another standout feature of the library's website is the seamless experience of having vendor platforms integrated into the library's website. Greenhill writes that "the embedded catalogue uses the <iframe> element to embed the Amlib web OPAC product with" a page of the website. The <iframe> HTML tag is probably familiar if you have ever embedded a YouTube video or a Google calendar in a website. Another example of an embedded item is the Flickr photo galleries.[8]

TEEN SUMMER CHALLENGE

http://teensummerchallenge.org/

The Teen Summer Challenge website from Pierce County Library Systems (PCLS) is a highly customized and successful site built around gamification. The "concept of applying game-design thinking to non-game applications," or gamification, is a growing trend in libraries, corporations, and has been used on the Web for years.[9] An example is when you fill out a profile on a website. Many sites will show you

143

a progress bar or give you suggestions like "upload your photo to increase your score by 10 points!" Businesses use gamification to increase customer interaction and awareness of their brand. PCLS's website uses gamification hallmarks such as badges, recent activity streams, and more to increase teen participation with the library's summer reading website. (Since gamification is projected to be used by over 50 percent of organizations by 2015, your library can also apply game mechanics to your online services; PCLS used WordPress's BuddyPress to do so.)[10] The initial impact of the PCLS site design is the bright yellow starburst background, which draws the eye to the content that is aligned in the center of the page. Along the top is the site's name, and the library's logo is helpfully placed in the top right as seen in the screen shot (fig. 13.2). The site's navigation runs horizontally under the header in drop-down menus. This way several menu options can be packed into the site for familiar users without sacrificing the clean look of the site. Log-in, registration, and search buttons are right-aligned in this menu bar. The footer includes links to the library, a thank-you message to the sponsors and community partners, and the library's contact information.

The star of the site: the actual gamification elements. These include colorful icons and badges. For each task successfully completed, the user is rewarded with one of these staff-made digital badges. Each user's profile lists their username, uploaded photo, and activity and achievements information, along with their list of friends. Each user can supply basic information, such as their favorite books and their hobbies. Perhaps most importantly for some users, their profile lists their point amounts and achievements. The site's success speaks for itself, as revealed in the "Evaluation" section.

Patrick McVicker, librarian at Pierce County Library System in Washington, answered the survey about his library's usage of WordPress.

The Library and Its Users

Pierce County is located in northwestern Washington State and is home to Mount Rainier. The service population was over 544,000 in 2011.[11] The library system includes eighteen branches. For the Teen Summer Challenge website, the site's target audience was for teens between 13 and 18 years of age (however, anyone can sign up to try out the website). Most teens of Pierce County can access the website from home, but a number use the site on their mobile device or through a computer at a library branch. The area's teens are very tech savvy, which matches data found in Pew Internet Research reports, McVicker notes. As teens may

FIGURE 13.2
Teen Summer Challenge site

not always have the interest or means to physically visit a library branch, having an interactive website was an ideal way to reach out to them for the summer program.

Why They Chose WordPress

WordPress's enthusiastic community has produced a number of plugins to modify the platform. For PCLS, that meant creating their new gamification website in-house on a well-supported platform. The other advantages of using WordPress included not having to pay for the software and previous experience with the software. All these factors were important in choosing a new direction for the yearly teen summer reading program. McVicker writes that teen participation had been "historically uninspiring." With a program ripe for an overhaul and the methodology of gamification at hand, it was time for staff to discuss the project. The Youth Services and Virtual Services departments met to hash out the details. It was decided that Youth Services would generate the content and plan the program. Meanwhile Virtual Services would handle "the development and design of the platform through which we'd make it all happen," McVicker writes.

Building with WordPress

McVicker himself did all the design and development work on the website. The total new expenses incurred by the website were $250 for the domain name as well as some themes and plugins that were used in the early stages. Site development moved quickly, with a prototype up and running within weeks after the decision was made to build the website. The site's development kicked off in December

2011 which led to a working site in March 2012. All library staff did extensive testing and usage of the site in May 2012. Satisfied that the site was ready for launch, PCLS used the website for the summer 2012 program. The website's first run lasted from June to September 2012, McVicker reports. The site's team stayed involved by engaging with site participants; their duties included awarding badges to winners and answering questions.

The website relies on a mix of forty-two different plugins for the site's functionality. A few of the plugins are outlined in the "Special Features" section below. Plugins also manage backing up the website through automated tasks.

Evaluation

While the summer program had not attracted teen involvement previously, the gamified WordPress website changed everything. Participants have provided enthusiastic feedback. However, the bigger story is within the numbers. Teen registration tripled compared to the previous year, and users "logged somewhere near 8,000 hours of engagement," McVicker reports. The Virtual Services team also found that the engagement on the Teen Summer Challenge's page views and visitors set a high benchmark for the library's main website to compete with. A final compelling number is that the average website visitor was spending twelve minutes and forty-two seconds on the special website. Therefore the teens were actively engaged chatting with one another, answering challenges, and overall participating in the Youth Services summer program.

Special Features

Building a gamification website takes some clever planning, but much of the heavy lifting can be done using three plugins. The first is BuddyPress, which adds "a lot of exciting community features for interaction," McVicker writes.[12] A few highlights of this plugin include allowing users to send private messages to each other, to have an activity stream (similar to a Facebook wall or Google Plus stream), and to display a list of friends.

The second plugin is the simple but effective Contact Form 7.[13] For the Teen Summer Challenge website, McVicker writes, Contact Form 7 "allowed us to manage the awarding of badges as well as provide easy feedback streams for users." Spam filters and CAPTCHA text can be enabled to ease the site manager's comment moderation duties. The plugin also supports advanced fields such as check boxes, radio buttons, and drop-down menus. The plugin then generates a line of code that you then paste into your post or page where the form will appear. With this amount of customization, you can probably create forms to replace embedded forms on your website completely!

To manage badges and the point system, PCLS relied on the Achievements for BuddyPress plugin.[14] Users gain visual prominence in the leaderboard and respect in the online community as they complete tasks. Each completed task earns a new badge and increases their score. For users who have a competitive bent, the Achievements plugin makes encouraging this competitive spirit even easier. Deciding when to reward a badge is set up in the plugin. Each achievement either is set as an award given directly by a site administrator or is automatically rewarded when specific criteria have been met. For instance, if a user's answers on the forum are voted as being helpful thirty times, the user would be awarded a most valuable player badge.

TOPEKA & SHAWNEE COUNTY PUBLIC LIBRARY

http://tscpl.org/

Major academic libraries often have very specialized staff who work on singular aspects of their website that run the gamut of website building. There can be a person just for user experience testing, someone to analyze web traffic, a designer, a content editor, and so on. For other library systems, convincing those in charge of budgets of the value of having a whole web department can be difficult. A great example of a public library with in-house designers and programmers is the Topeka

& Shawnee County Public Library (TSCPL). Their website is so customized that at first glance, it bears none of the hallmarks of being powered by WordPress! Therefore the library has been able to create an online presence that is custom fit to the needs of their community using WordPress and their own in-house web team.

TSCPL packs a lot of content onto their home page, as seen in the screen shot (fig. 13.3). At the top is a header that features their library's logo, a photo of the building, a search box, and user-centric navigation buttons (Catalog, My Account, Get A Library Card, and Donate Now). A second horizontal navigation bar sits below with links to different information about the library itself. These links about the library's offerings drop down to mega menus when clicked.[15] (A mega menu is a drop-down menu that usually has the benefit of not "going back up" if the user moves their mouse from it. This is a great for people who have trouble using a mouse.) The focal point of the home page is a WP Featured Content Slider to highlight the library's big events.[16] Other features on the homepage include banners for longer-term events (e.g., an art show), a virtual book display of six selected titles, several call-to-action buttons (e.g., chat with a librarian and subscription links), links to new posts, and a custom calendar. The above content is sorted into a main column and then a right sidebar. The footer is dedicated to the library's social media efforts with a Facebook link, the latest Twitter tweet, Pinterest pins, the newest uploaded YouTube video, and Flickr photos. At the very bottom of the page is the library's contact information. Posts on the website are categorized and tagged; each category has a customized appearance similar to the list of posts on the home page. Individual posts include metadata in the right sidebar with information about the post's date, category (e.g., blog), tags, and a brief post author biography.

David Lee King, digital services director at Topeka & Shawnee County Public Library, answered the survey about his library's usage of WordPress.[17]

The Library and Its Users

Situated on the eastern side of Kanas, Topeka is home to just over 128,000 people, according to the 2011 estimate by the U.S. Census Bureau.[18] Of these 128,000 residents, over 96,000 of them are also card-carrying members of TSCPL.[19] Aside from having a building in central Topeka, the library also owns two bookmobiles that serve eighteen locations.

The members of this public library range in age from 4 to 80 years old. Users have a range of technical skills and access the Web from home or office. Internet connections are made from connected broadband, wireless, and 3G. With such a

FIGURE 13.3
Topeka and Shawnee County Public Library site

diversity of user ability and access, TSCPL knew that they needed to build a library website that is easy to understand and navigate no matter your skill level.

Why They Chose WordPress

In 2010, the staff at TSCPL met to discuss building a new website. King describes their three objectives for the website as making it easier to use, shortening the length of their homepage, and clearly distinguishing between permanent information (e.g., library hours) and time-sensitive information (e.g., events). TSCPL's web decision makers were King, the management team, and the administration team. They chose to use WordPress because it's "easier to code and customize, has a large user community (i.e. millions for WordPress vs. thousands for Drupal), and is easier to train non-techie staff to use," King writes.

Building with WordPress

The new website was launched in early 2011. All the site's design and configuration was produced in-house. Of the nine months it took to build the website, three months were spent perfecting the website's design. TSCPL did extensive user testing: they would create a design, solicit feedback, integrate the suggestions into their design, and then show it to users again. At the end the web team produced the site we see today—100 percent customized. As part of this process, the library produced their own theme, called TSCPL. Additionally, the library integrated their Polaris catalog into the website through their custom plugin, TSCPL Polaris.

While creating a customized installation of WordPress was possible thanks to the library's in-house designers and programmers, the website also uses a number of free publicly available plugins. One of them, Yoast WordPress SEO, improves search engine rankings.[20] WP Page Numbers controls the display of post navigation on the bottom of lists as numbers (instead of using *next* and *previous*.)[21] This plugin can be seen on the bottom of the home page. For the attention-grabbing slideshow on the home page, the library relies on the widespread WP Featured Content Slider.[22] For the library's popular community podcast discussions, the website uses the Audio Player plugin.[23]

Every day the website is updated with new content by library staff. To protect valuable data, the website is hosted on the library's own Linux server which is located onsite. Additionally, the server is backed up each night. WordPress's core and plugins are updated by two web staff, King reports. For more information about creating the website, read "Our Website Redesign is Live!" post on King's blog.[24]

Evaluation

King notes that the library has never received any complaints about the new website. This is outstanding considering the diversity of their 96,000 user population's tech skills and age ranges. Currently the web team is gathering user feedback by e-mail and word of mouth. The contact forms on the website are provided through Gravity Forms.[25] This premium plugin can schedule when forms open and expire, report how many submissions are accepted, show a progress indicator, and more.

Special Features

While TSCPL has the advantage of specially skilled staff, there are features of their website that can be replicated at other libraries without advanced support. TSCPL makes heavy use of built-in WordPress widgets for their site sidebar. Each widget includes CSS to divide the text widget into a header section and then the widget's main text or image display. For example, the "Library News connectnow" section is made up of a header that lists the widget's title and a link to the tag *connectnow*. Then the widget's main content is a simple image that has been coded in with a link to the library's virtual magazine (powered by Issuu).

Another example of a text widget is the Ask Now chat box and contact information on the top of the sidebar. By clicking on the graphic image of a button, a pop-up window appears to start a conversation with a staff member. The default text widget provided by WordPress does not accept the Javascript needed for the pop-up chat box, but you can add this feature with the Enhanced Text Widget plugin.[26] Simply download, install, and activate this plugin to get started. You then drag the new widget into your site's widget location before typing your code in.

A final feature that can be reproduced by anyone is the library's mega menu. While the library manually created their mega menu navigation using jQuery, a Javascript library, you can do something similar with the jQuery Mega Menu plugin.[27] Install and activate the plugin as normal, then drag the new widget into your theme. To create the mega menu, you will need to have made custom menus that are three levels deep. For example, your menu could be for programming at your library. A single menu item could have Events as the parent, Age Groups as the second level, then particular program types for that age group as the final level:

Events --> Children --> Storytimes

If your mega menu does not show up, check your website's theme template files. More information can be found on the plugin creator's website.[28]

WEST DES MOINES LIBRARY *CHILDREN'S BLOG*

www.wdmlibrarykids.com

Early literacy is the star of the West Des Moines Library (WDMPL) *Children's Blog*. The website informs parents about early literacy skills, demonstrates how parents and librarians can work together to teach children, and includes in-depth guides on what literacy skills to tackle at different phases of development from babies to preschoolers. Additionally, the site hosts a blog for the children's librarians, a calendar of programs, multiple subscription options, and testimonials from patrons. Most of the content on the website started its life as resources being shared in person with patrons. However, as the resources expanded beyond what could reasonably be included in a pamphlet, the library's rich trove has been made available online.

The website's information is a fixed-width site centered in the web browser window and features a playful background illustration of a sun, clouds, a rainbow, and a winding road through a forest. When the web browser is expanded across two monitors, this background image changes in scale to match the new width. This is a fun detail that adds to the delight of the WDMPL's website. Inspiring feelings of enjoyment and good surprises improves a user's experience, as explained in Aarron Walter's *Designing for Emotion* (A Book Apart, 2011). WDMPL carries this playful attitude throughout the rest of their website as well. Bright colors draw attention to the top horizontal navigation and the additional right vertical navigation on the home page. Buttons are also colorful and are designed with gradients and helpful arrows to help communicate that a click here will perform an action. Additionally, a slider on the home page highlights five feature stories about early literacy, as seen in the screen shot (fig. 13.4). Images are used for activities such as registering online for events and searching the library's catalog. Individual pages feature a large title and headers—which makes for easier scanning for a caregiver with a wiggly child on their lap. A right sidebar navigation points to early literacy resources based upon age. Posts are also tagged and include a comment box for quick feedback. The footer includes the library's contact information and hours, links to downloadable materials, a link to the Friends website, social media icons, and a search box.

Nate Huber, children's librarian at West Des Moines Library in Iowa, answered the survey about his department's usage of WordPress.

The Library and Its Users

West Des Moines is located just south of the central part of Iowa. The library serves a population of nearly 58,000 residents.[29] Huber writes, "Socioeconomically, we serve people everywhere on the spectrum," so patrons have a diverse amount of familiarity with technology. The target population for the blog is mothers and

FIGURE 13.4
West Demoines Library Children's Blog site

153

caregivers. This group of users tends to be more tech savvy than the general population, but Huber notes that most patrons have basic computer skills and have access to the Internet on a home computer. The library's vision statement promotes a joy of reading, a love of learning, and sharing knowledge, which the library's *Children's Blog* fulfills.[30]

Why They Chose WordPress

Early literacy has been a vital part of the programming at WDMPL for years. When the Every Child Ready to Read campaign started to take root in libraries, Huber proposed to the other WDMPL librarians that they should promote their already successful early literacy program on the Web.[31] With materials and ECRR's tools online, parents and caregivers could access early literacy materials at their own point of need. Plus, a website would make the library's resources more accessible, more organized, and easier to share. So WDMPL began their research by surveying other local libraries to see who had placed their early literacy programs online; none had. Therefore the librarians came to a consensus that they "wanted to be the first in our area" to offer early literacy information online, Huber writes.

Huber's prior experience with WordPress made it an easy CMS to recommend for the library's new website. When talking to staff, he discussed how the software "was easy to use, has almost endless customization, incorporated the features we wanted, looked professional, and it is a free/open source platform where improvements are always being made." Once the staff had all agreed to the new initiative, it was time to talk to the administration. With the administrators on board, it was then off to chat with the Friends of the Library for some additional funding for domain and hosting fees.

154

Building with WordPress

Producing a successful website does not come about without some hurdles. For WDMPL, the first struggle was to get complete buy-in from the department that an active and relevant website could be developed and maintained. Furthermore, it was important that content had "a distinct voice, that voice fit our community, the information was easy to understand, and we did not overwhelm people with information," Huber notes. The website has achieved these goals by using natural language in short sentences and bulleted lists to get points across quickly. The content was developed by the entire department's staff (Jenna Ehler, Betsy Richter, Jennifer Cisar, and Huber). However, even working together toward a rewarding outcome for their community did not come without its stresses. Staff had to do their content research, development, writing, and then rewriting around their already full schedules. Content continues to be maintained by staff, while the website's updates are done by Huber.

Aside from content, the website itself had to be built by Huber. He had spent a year shopping around the idea of creating an early literacy blog before the department decided to do it. Once all parties were in agreement, Huber finally broke ground on the website a month later. The first websites used the free Twenty Eleven theme.[32] Then in the fall of 2012, the library purchased themeforest's Pekaboo theme, which provides by default the website's background, colorful buttons, and overall playful appearance.[33] By choosing such a great theme—which includes all these wonderful design elements straight out of the box—WDMPL saved design development time in exchange for a small fee. Web hosting and domain names were purchased through Blue Host.[34] Huber relies on Blue Host for the site's automatic backups.

Evaluation

While their website is a great early literacy resource, Huber notes that they are "a little late to the game in implementing a blog." Patrons do not expect the Children's Library to have a website, so staff has to continue to raise awareness. However, those who do visit have verbally expressed a positive experience. Google Analytics reveals that there are consistently fifty unique visitors each week, and the bounce rate of people who visit just one page and then leave is only 1 percent. This is a phenomenally low bounce rate (the average is 50 percent[35]). So while traffic is currently low, the patrons who visit are fully engaged and learning from the content on the WDMPL website.

155

Special Features

Because content is king, WDMPL needs to make sure theirs is as accessible as possible. To push new information to busy caregivers who may forget to come back and visit the site, WDMPL uses the Subscription Options plugin.[36] This plugin is a widget, so you just drag it to the appropriate widget area in your theme. Then, for each supported service, you add your library's URL for that platform. Simple!

With so much content, you need to make sure that your page is loading fast. WDMPL relies on the W3 Total Cache plugin. Website caches "store copies of documents" so that the server is not being repeatedly asked to process pages that have not changed since a previous visit.[37] (Caches are beneficial in Google searches when a website has changed or gone down, but you can click the cache to see what a page looked like when Google's robot last visited it. In this way, a cache is somewhat like a temporary time capsule.) For your site's purposes, the fewer times your server has to serve up content, the faster your site will run overall.

An advantage of WordPress is that it is simple to use a plugin that is meeting your needs now, and and simple to discontinue using it if your website changes. WDMPL was using the Websimon Tables plugin for their Early Literacy navigation.[38] When the website switched to its new theme, Websimon became redundant and was removed. Likewise, WDMPL has also earmarked a plugin to try when they update their ILS, the OpenBook Book Data plugin.[39] The advantage of this plugin is that it would save staff data entry time because it automatically pulls in a book's cover, author, publication information, and so on from the Open Library.[40] So be flexible in your site's development—but remember that fewer plugins are better than too many!

WILTON LIBRARY ASSOCIATION

There are many ways to distribute, share, and check a library's internal policies. Traditional methods include handbooks, message boards, or simply a stack of printed pages kept (and lost!) in a desk drawer. However, finding then searching through shared staff documents is a tedious process. Not to mention then running down to the copier to make a copy! At the Wilton Library Association (WLA), they decided to take their internal staff documents, policies, and information and make it available through their own intranet. Using WordPress, the intranet is a private, internal website that only staff has access to.[41] Using this distribution method, staff are only a few keystrokes away from the latest procedures, tutorials, and more. The best part is that the content is always up to date without the need to print off dozens of copies when there is a revision.

Since the WLA site is internal, there is no website for the public visit and examine. Instead, a description of the current site will have to suffice. The site uses a customized version of the Twenty Eleven theme with the sidebars removed. Therefore, the site navigation is located solely across the top, as seen in the screen shot (fig. 13.5). Each menu item in this horizontal list reveals a drop-down menu when hovered or clicked upon. The site's content is written using only pages. The header consists of the WLA's logo with five rotating images. The footer contains a copyright statement and the library's address.

Mary Anne Mendola Franco, head of Network Services at Wilton Library Association in Connecticut, answered the survey about her library's usage of WordPress.

The Library and Its Users

WLA employs about forty-five librarians and staff members. The staff's age range mirrors the patron population from teenagers to those in their 80s. Wilton empowers their staff to learn new technologies through continuous training sessions. Departments are encouraged to maintain their own pages on the website.

Home   Departments   Information   Tools   🔎 Search

WLA Intranet

~ Updated July 20, 2012 ~
Staff news for the week of July 22 – 28

{Rotation B2}

Department head meeting on Tuesday at 12:15 pm in the Presidents' Room. **Staff training** on Thursday at 9:00 am in the Rimer Room.

The **"Caught You Reading" Teen Photo Contest** will accept submissions until July 23 at the Circulation Desk.

Library programs this week: Drop-in summer crafts for kids all day on Monday; Reception for Weir Farm Artists-in-Residence Leona and Richard Frank on Monday at 7:00 pm; Story times for kids throughout the day on Tuesday; OverDrive "Office Hours" on Tuesday from 4-6:00 pm AND Saturday from 10-12:00 pm; Medieval Lute program for kids on Wednesday at 3:00 pm; Teens learn how to make movies on Xtranormal on Wednesday at 3:00 pm; Solar Energy workshop on Wednesday from 7-9:00 pm; Firefly Jar Craft for teens on Thursday from 3-5:00 pm; Kids Knit on Thursday at 4:00 pm; Summer Music and More concert series concludes on Thursday at 5:00 pm; Medieval Movies for kids on Friday at 10:15 am; Friday Flicks for kids at 2:00 pm; Kids' Garden Club meets on Friday at 4:00 pm; Tales to Tails on Saturday at 11:00 am.

Current art exhibit: The 68th Annual Summer Art Show exhibition will be hung on July 5 and will run through August 31. The reception for this exhibit was held on Friday, July 6.

Unshelved   by Bill Barnes and Gene Ambaum

© 1997-2012 Wilton Library Association
137 Old Ridgefield Road, Wilton, CT 06897
203-762-3950 (p) ~ 203-834-1166 (f)

FIGURE 13.5
Wilton Library Association site

Why They Chose WordPress

The need for an intranet became obvious to WLA in the 1990s. Franco writes, "Our intranet was conceived with the idea of having necessary information for staff reside in one convenient place." The first intranet was built in 1999 using HomeSite.[42] Then, in 2004/2005, the WLA switched to using Contribute and Dreamweaver for website development.[43] However, when a new external website was developed for the library in WordPress in 2010, it was decided to move the intranet to WordPress as well to achieve a "unified platform for both applications," Franco writes. Decisions for both sites were made by the executive director, the head of network services, and the webmaster. When deciding on the new CMS, the library looked primarily for the ability to create and manage content with ease.

Building with WordPress

Since the WLA already had an intranet in place and a new library website that used WordPress, the process of building the new intranet went smoother than if the WLA were starting from scratch. First, the webmaster had to decide what theme to use for the intranet. He settled on creating a child theme for the popular Twenty Eleven theme.[44] A child theme uses custom CSS to transform the look of the original parent theme. The beauty of this is that by keeping your custom code separate, when the parent theme is updated, you will not lose all your changes. However, you may have to modify your child theme to take advantage of new features in the parent theme.

Next, the webmaster had to move the intranet's content. This job was pretty easy, as content only had to be copied into WordPress pages. However, work also had to be done to change the links to point to the new pages as needed. The information architecture was set up "in response to how our staff answers questions," Franco writes. The home page is the most actively updated page on the intranet. Each week, the intranet is updated with a list of staff birthdays and important news concerning library activities by the head of Technical Services. For fun, a RSS feed of the library-themed web comic Unshelved is on the front page as well.[45] A more serious side of the site content includes staff meeting minutes and links to the control panels of various printers. So, while the content on the Intranet could be strictly policy-related stuff, the ability to access dynamic, practical information about the printers makes the intranet invaluable for tech staff. With this advantage, the tech staff can diagnosis and fix problems no matter where they are in the building.

Since the WLA already had a strong history of using the Web for their communications, no new resources were required. The library already had a server to install WordPress on. Also, the webmaster was a preexisting position, so no new staff needed to be hired. For the library's new website, they hired an outside designer. This person used the Cutline 1.3 theme for the main library website.[46]

The intranet, as intended, continues to be a living document. New content updates and design refinements are done by the webmaster. Several staff members have the ability to post on their own department pages with the role of editor. Other staff members can send new content to the webmaster for uploading. The site is backed up daily along with the library's website. Additional support for the management of the intranet is provided to the webmaster through the head of Technical Services; she updates the weekly content on the front page of the intranet.

Evaluation

Taking on the task of maintaining a website is a big responsibility. The WLA approaches both their library website and intranet thoughtfully. Franco explains, "We are always striving to improve the website and intranet in response to best practices, patron and staff input, advances in technology, and the desire to give our community good, reliable, current, accurate, and authoritative information." The community for the intranet is of course the staff, who use it frequently. With a "one-stop shop" mentality, staff are never more than a few feet away from an intranet-linked computer that keeps them in the loop on the latest library developments. As for statistics, none are kept for the intranet; the WLA does note that their library website receives visits long after the library has closed for the day.

Special Features

In order to build the navigation system, the WLA webmaster employed custom menus. While the default menu system would work in theory, it is easier to use the custom menus option so that pages can be rearranged through a drag-and-drop interface. The WLA intranet uses four custom menus. The first includes the pages for "Home," "Departments," "Information," and "Tools." The other three menus are assigned to one item in the first menu. So for instance, the "Departments" custom menu displays links to "Reference," "Children," "Teens," and so on.

To add custom menus to your website, go to your WordPress dashboard, then click on Appearance, then Menus. On the right side of the screen, create a new custom menu by first giving it a title. You can add content for the menu by looking to the column on the left. Some of the options include custom links (which are usually not linking to content that is on your WordPress website), choose pages, or certain categories. Notice that posts are not listed here because they are usually not items that go in a menu. To link to a post, just use the Custom Links widget. Once your menu item is populated with links, hit Save. To the left, you will see the Theme Locations area. Choose the location where you want your custom menu to appear. These locations are determined by your theme. Hit Save again. Check your website to make sure the custom menu is displaying. To rearrange the items in your custom menu, simply left-click and continue to hold down the mouse button. Then drag the menu item above or below other items. If you want to indent a menu item as the child of another item, just drag the item below the parent and then further to the right; you will see the new child item move over. Please note that how your custom menus display is completely dependent upon your theme.

ADDITIONAL LIBRARIES

Darien Library

http://kidlibcamp.darien.org/

Previously, a wiki had been used to collect discussions held at the library's annual KidLibCamp unconference. In 2012, the library used two WordPress websites for their camp. The main website is hosted by WordPress, while the second site here is a forum addition.[47] The plugin used for this collaborative space is Mingle Forum.[48]

Disclaimer: I put together this forum website in about an hour and modified the website's theme to match the original website more closely.

New York Public Library

http://candide.nypl.org/text/

The Candide 2.0: Networked Edition project is a way for users to discuss particular passages of Voltaire's book. Each paragraph can be clicked and a comment left on just that section. The unique commenting system is powered by the Digress.it plugin.[49] The front page's navigation is color coded, showing which chapters have been annotated.

NOTES

1. Krug, Steve. *Don't Make Me Think: A Common Sense Approach to Web Usability*. Berkeley, CA: New Riders, 2006.

2. Sayontan Sinha, "Suffusion," http://wordpress.org/extend/themes/suffusion.

3. Greenhill blogs at http://kathryngreenhill.com/.

4. Australia Bureau of Statistics, "3218.0 – Regional Population Growth, Australia, 2010-11," 2012, www.abs.gov.au/ausstats/abs@.nsf/Products/3218.0~2010-11~Main+Features~Western+Australia?OpenDocument#PARALINK5.

5. The Grove Library, "About Us," http://thegrovelibrary.net/about-5/about-us/.

6. Kathryn Greenhill, "Why I Am Using Suffusion WordPress Theme for Our Library Website," 2010, www.librariansmatter.com/blog/2010/06/29/why-i-am-using-suffusion-wordpress-theme-for-our-library-website/.

7. Nicky F. Simpson, "cformsII," www.deliciousdays.com/cforms-plugin/. A January 2009 discussion on the WordPres Tavern forum states that the removal was due to a licensing issue between the plugin creator and WordPress's Open Source terms (www.wptavern.com/forum/plugins-hacks/84-cforms-ii-removed-repository.html). Additional information on the plugin's website states, "Heck, it's even released under GPL now!" (www.deliciousdays.com/cforms-plugin/), which uses the same licensing agreement as WordPress. However, the plugin has not returned to WordPress's official plugin repository.

8. The Grove Library, "Photo Gallery," http://thegrovelibrary.net/the-building/photo-gallery/.

9. "Gamification Wiki," http://gamification.org/.

10. Gartner Inc., "Gartner Says By 2015, More Than 50 Percent of Organizations That Manage Innovation Processes Will Gamify Those Processes," 2011, www.gartner.com/it/page.jsp?id=1629214.

11. Pierce County Library System, "Fast Facts," www.piercecountylibrary.org/about-us/about-overview/fast-facts.htm.

12. BuddyPress is a program that is derived from WordPress. It is compatible with WordPress and its plugins are available on the Plugin Directory. The Teen Summer Challenge uses BuddyPress. John James Jacoby, Paul Gibbs, and Boone Gorges, "BuddyPress," http://wordpress.org/extend/plugins/buddypress/.

13. Takayukister, "Contact Form 7," http://wordpress.org/extend/plugins/contact-form-7/.

14. Paul Gibbs, "Achievements for BuddyPress," http://wordpress.org/extend/plugins/achievements/.

15. Hana Jung, "Trendspotting: Mega-Menus," 2012, www.browsermedia.com/blog/2012/05/23/trendspotting-mega-menus.

16. Iwebix and Dennis Nissle, "WP Featured Content Slider," http://wordpress.org/extend/plugins/wp-featured-content-slider/.

17. King blogs at www.davidleeking.com.

18. United States Census Bureau, "State & County QuickFacts: Topeka (city), Kansas," http://quickfacts.census.gov/qfd/states/20/2071000.html.

19. Topeka & Shawnee County Public Library, "2013 Budget Summary," paper presented at the annual public meeting for Topeka & Shawnee County Public Library, Topeka, Kansas, August 9, 2012.

20. Joost de Valk, "WordPress SEO by Yoast," http://wordpress.org/extend/plugins/wordpress-seo/.

21. jenst, "WP Page Numbers," http://wordpress.org/extend/plugins/wp-page-numbers/.

22. Iwebix and Dennis Nissle, "WP Featured Content Slider," http://wordpress.org/extend/plugins/wp-featured-content-slider/.

23. doryphores, "Audio Player," http://wordpress.org/extend/plugins/audio-player/.

24. David Lee King, "Our Website Redesign is Live!" March 2, 2011, www.davidleeking.com/2011/03/02/our-website-redesign-is-live/#.UOYjO28701J.

25. Gravity, "Gravity Forms," www.gravityforms.com.

26. bostondv, "Enhanced Text Widget," http://wordpress.org/extend/plugins/enhanced-text-widget/.

27. jQuery, http://jquery.com/; Remix, "JQuery Mega Menu Widget," http://wordpress.org/extend/plugins/jquery-mega-menu/.

28. Design Chemical, "WordPress Plugins Frequently Asked Questions – jQuery Mega Menu," www.designchemical.com/blog/index.php/frequently-asked-questions/jquery-mega-menu/.

29. United States Census Bureau, "State & County QuickFacts: West Des Moines (city), Iowa," http://quickfacts.census.gov/qfd/states/19/1983910.html.

30. Wes Des Moines Public Library, "Vision Statement," 2010, www.wdmlibrary.org/aspx/information.aspx?s=6&c=19.

31. Every Child Ready to Read @ your library, http://everychildreadytoread.org/.

32. wordpressdotorg, "Twenty Eleven," http://wordpress.org/extend/themes/twentyeleven.

33. themeforest, "Pekaboo for WordPress – Children Theme Template," http://themeforest.net/item/pekaboo-for-wordpress-children-theme-template/409980.

34. Blue Host, www.bluehost.com.

35. Kayden Kelly, "What Is Bounce Rate? Avoid Common Pitfalls," February 12, 2012, Blast Advanced Media, www.blastam.com/blog/index.php/2012/02/what-is-bounce-rate/; Matt Quinn, "How to Reduce Your Website's Bounce Rate," January 31, 2011, Inc., www.inc.com/guides/2011/01/how-to-reduce-your-website-bounce-rate.html.

36. Tom Saunter, "Subscription Options," http://wordpress.org/extend/plugins/subscription-options/.

37. Frederick Townes, "W3 Total Cache," http://wordpress.org/extend/plugins/w3-total-cache/; Wikipedia, "Web Cache," http://en.wikipedia.org/wiki/Web_cache.

38. Websimon, "Websimon Tables," http://wordpress.org/extend/plugins/websimon-tables/.

39. John Miedema, "OpenBook Book Data," http://wordpress.org/extend/plugins/openbook-book-data/.

40. Open Library, http://openlibrary.org/.

41. Wikipedia, "Intranet," http://en.wikipedia.org/wiki/Intranet.

42. Wikipedia, "Macromedia HomeSite," http://en.wikipedia.org/wiki/Macromedia_HomeSite.

43. Adobe, "Contribute 6.5," www.adobe.com/products/contribute.html; Adobe, "Adobe Dreamweaver CS6," www.adobe.com/products/dreamweaver.html.

44. wordpressdotorg, "Twenty Eleven," http://wordpress.org/extend/themes/twentyeleven.

45. Unshelved, www.unshelved.com.

46. Splashpress Media, "Cutline Theme for WordPress," http://cutline.tubetorial.com/.

47. KidLibCamp, http://kidlibcamp.wordpress.com.

48. Cartpauj, "Mingle Forum," http://wordpress.org/extend/plugins/mingle-forum/.

49. visudo, "Digress.it," http://wordpress.org/extend/plugins/digressit/.

Chapter Fourteen

School Library Media Centers

BELCHERTOWN HIGH SCHOOL LIBRARY

http://bhslib.wordpress.com/

For a school library, it is easy to build a website whose target audience is just the student body. In my research for this book, I visited hundreds of school websites, and there was often not even a passing nod to the other users of the library—the school's faculty and staff. However, at the Belchertown High School Library, the librarian has also built-in support for the teachers that he works closely with. He provides resources about lesson planning, the state's standards, and more on a link clearly marked Teachers. While the website also shines for its collection of study guides and encouragement of mobile databases, it is the attention paid to the whole service population that makes this school library website shine.

The library relies on WordPress.com to host their website and currently uses the beautiful Oxygen theme by DevPress.[1] This theme is responsive, which means the website will look great no matter what device the population uses to access the library's online presence. Another showstopper of the theme is the featured images that appear on the front page's slideshow, as seen in the screen shot (fig. 14.1). The library uses this slideshow to feature new posts, including suggestions for newer technologies such as Google Drive. Content on the home page is always fresh, and the eye-catching images draw interest to these new posts. Navigation runs horizontally across the top and down the side. The top navigation is the website's pages and include links to the study guides, teacher's section, library

FIGURE 14.1
Belchertown High School Library

polices, and so on. The left sidebar includes catalog and database links. The sidebar also includes quick links to frequently asked topics such as MLA Citation Help, a calendar, and an RSS feed to the New York Times News. The left sidebar is a widget from Goodreads that displays six book covers at a time of books the librarian has recently reviewed.[2] The center content on the home page is the aforementioned slider as well as links to other recent articles. The newer articles have images, while further down the page, the older articles do not display an accompanying picture. In the footer is a statement of who owns the website and who is responsible for the site's maintenance. Individual posts and pages keep the left and right sidebars but gain a social sharing footer. However, comments are not allowed on the website.

Brennan Murray, library media specialist at the Belchertown High School Library in Massachusetts, answered the survey about his library's usage of WordPress.

The Library and Its Users

Belchertown High School Library is located in Belchertown, Massachusetts, which is just south of being in the center of the state. The school's service population consists of approximately eight hundred students and seventy faculty and staff members. Bullying is taken very seriously in this school district, as each school's website provides ways to report bullying incidents. Murray notes that their student access to Internet at home and tech savviness is mixed. Belchertown is close to Amherst, so the students come from both rural and upper-middle-class demographics, which creates a diverse set of tech access and familiarity across the student body.

Why They Choose WordPress

Murray was hired as the school's library media specialist in 2009. The website needed a redesign to include better "flexibility and Web 2.0 integration for the site to keep it relevant and timely," Murray states. He consulted with the school's technology department to get the all-clear on using WordPress. Once approved, Murray built the site entirely by himself. His experience with WordPress was earned while doing projects in graduate school. He writes that he loves "how user-friendly the platform is, while allowing the users a wide range of powerful options." During seminars with teachers, he also advocates the ease of creating websites in WordPress for anyone who can write e-mail messages and who is familiar with Microsoft Word.

Building with WordPress

Once the decision was made to build a website, it took Murray only a month to put the site together. His choice for using the hosted WordPress was a decision based upon needing a reliable server. The local school district had run into some server issues, so the library needed a better option. Of course, the ability to put together a website without adding to the library's finances was a great selling point.

The website is completely managed by Murray. While he trusts WordPress .com's servers, he does a periodic backup of his website's database. Murray does not worry about updates, because they are managed by WordPress.com as part of being a hosted website.

As far as the website's milestones, the successful launch of the new website was the biggest moment. Murray web design philosophy is that the website is "never fully complete, and should always be improved and added to in order to keep content fresh." So his job is never-ending. (During the writing of this book, he completely revamped the site's design—further proof that he takes his job as librarian/webmaster very seriously.)

Evaluation

As stated in the introduction for this website, this school library cares about their entire service population. Murray uses statistical analysis and gathers feedback to see how well the library is doing in meeting their goal to "serve the information needs of our student and faculty population." When he looks over the reports and responses, he then adjusts the website as needed for an improved experience. For example, Murray checks what keywords are being searched for on the website. If the website has no information on that topic, the library will then update the website to add the sought-for content. This responsiveness and analysis also tips the library off on what new resources students are looking for as they choose their research topics. Murray also notes that the site is visited when school is out, which means his library is competitive against big search engines for their local patron base.

Special Features

Content rules the Belchertown High School Library website. Students have easy access to the project help guides for different teachers. Each guide is a page, which is divided into sections that match the teacher's needs. Then each resource is a link either that students can access on the open Web or that goes to a library-provided database. A few of these guides include relevant images. By having these guides online, the school can save on printing costs (and students pulling a last-minute all-nighter can get the resources they need for their project straight from their library, which already knows what materials they need to succeed).

Second, the library's website recognizes that students are using mobile devices to access content. The website's new theme is attractive and adjusts according to the viewport of the device that is accessing the website. While a visually appealing website may sound minor, a responsive website that adjusts its appearance for the user's device is an accessibility issue: pinching and zooming to see a full-sized, desktop-optimized website on a tiny screen can be physically and visually difficult for some users. As well, this library promotes the use of mobile apps to their students by placing the link to mobile apps second in their navigation. Students are encouraged to use apps to easily access the catalog, databases, and Overdrive's e-books and audiobooks. Students at Belchertown are being prepped for the adult world by using tools provided by the library that they will use every day in the years to come.

ESCALANTE VALLEY ELEMENTARY SCHOOL

http://escalantevalley.wordpress.com/

For many schools, their library's websites are handled by IT staff or by a district home office with little control by the library. At Escalante Valley Elementary School, the librarian created and manages two websites that she built with WordPress: the school's main website and a site for the library. The school's website is self-hosted, while the library uses WordPress.com. The librarian's role of also managing the parent institution's website makes it unique among libraries. The focus of this section is on the library's own website, but mentions of the school website will be included as well.[3]

Patrons often eagerly share with librarians and library staff how they are using library resources to learn, discover, and create new objects. So while librarians know that their materials are being put to creating new things, the library is usually not involved any further, as the produced item is not shared with the rest of the community. The patron's excitement and great work then slip away unnoticed by their neighbors. However, some libraries are channeling their patrons' creativity by setting up "maker spaces," which gives their patrons a place to create new analog and digital items within the library. At the Chicago Public Library's YOUmedia teen space, patron work is then shared via an online magazine.[4] However, your library does not need to have a creative engine like a maker space to inspire patrons to create and share their work with the community. The Escalante Valley Media Center in Utah displays their elementary students' work on their WordPress website. The website promotes projects that students created based on the topics they learn about from the library's resources.

FIGURE 14.2
Escalante Valley Elmentary School

The Escalante Valley Media Center uses WordPress.com for their website with the Chateau theme by Ignacio Ricci. A large word cloud called a Wordle dominates the top of the website, highlighting terms related to the importance of twenty-first-century learning, as seen in the screen shot (fig. 14.2).[5] In the left sidebar, the library includes a category cloud (similar to a tag cloud), a list of local and educational resource blogs, links to book and tutorial sites, and links to library resources. The website is set up in a default blog layout with reverse chronological posts. Each post uses photos featuring projects created by the students from library resources (e.g., the human body) or students using library resources such as an iPad. Comments and social media sharing buttons are enabled on the posts. In the website's footer, an e-mail subscription link helps followers keep up with the library's postings.

Chris Haught, librarian and media specialist at Escalante Valley Media Center in Utah, answered the survey about her library's usage of WordPress.

The Library and Its Users

Escalante Valley Elementary School is located in Beryl, Utah, which is in the southwestern corner of the state. The school is located in a rural farming community. There are six teachers to instruct the 141 preK–grade 6 student body. This unincorporated town is not recognized by the federal census data, so further population data is not readily available.[6] Because Beryl is a farming community, students' families may be migrant workers or own their own farm. This means that the school has a "higher than average ratio of low income families, compared to other schools in our district," Haught writes. Despite this, Haught notes that a recent informal survey revealed that aside from school access, 80 percent of the students have access to the Internet thanks to the advent of smartphones.

Why They Chose WordPress

Since Beryl, Utah, is so rural; the principal had a vision to make sure to prepare students for a world outside their small community. As part of this five-year plan, technology was chosen to be highlighted as a vital part of the students' school lives. The website the school sought to create would allow students to share their work with the outside world—a world where students "had no concept of the differences between rural, suburban and urban communities," Haught describes. Before building the two websites, Haught had been the webmaster for the school's website, where she had used Joomla. However, when the school district announced that they would no longer support Joomla, Haught suggested moving to WordPress because she had used it successfully for other projects. When she became the school's technology specialist, Haught then recommended moving both the school's website and the library's website to WordPress. The new library website was approved by the principal and technology director. The new website also had the support and input from the school's faculty and staff.

Building with WordPress

Once Haught had approval, she set to work on the new library website. With WordPress's ease of use, she was able to put the site together within twenty minutes.

Content was provided over time and has been added by not only Haught but also by the students. For Haught, a verification that the library is meeting the principal's vision to integrate technology into students' lives is when student work is posted on the website and students are able to share their projects with distant family members. These projects are "the culmination of learning based projects" that the library's resources helped them to create, Haught writes. While the sharing aspect of the website is cool for the students, Haught notes that "the process of creating the projects is where the learning really happened."

For the school's website, Haught was able to use her knowledge as a hosting reseller (a person who purchase a bulk amount of server space, then sells portion of it to individuals) to purchase the school's domain and host it. Haught notes that their school's method may be "not the best option for most schools [...] but this worked well for us." The site's updates and backups are done using Manage WordPress.[7] News-driven items dominate the school's website with reports about events happening in the classroom and student participation in local science fairs. Haught configured the school's website in an hour. Each teacher in the school is able to post content under their own category. For the site's theme, Haught purchased a premium WordPress theme, WP-DaVinci 20 by Solostream.[8] A highlight of this theme is the built-in slider, which is used on the school's homepage.

Evaluation

For Haught, one of the benefits of the websites is being able to use them as direct resources for questions. That is, when someone wants to know about the school or library she has a set place to send them to for more information. The school has noticed that students "tend to put more effort into work they know is going to be seen by others," Haught writes. Students are also actively engaged with sharing their work—they want to see the site's statistics and whether anyone has left them comments. For a very small community, these two websites allow them to start interacting with the world at large.

Special Features

Because Haught is a webmaster not just for her media center, but also for the the entire school and many personal projects, she needed some help in keeping each WordPress installation updated. To accomplish this, she uses ManageWP, which is a paid service. Haught writes that this "allows me to consolidate all my websites

(20) into one dashboard" where she can update all the website's plugins and themes from one interface. Other features of the service include additional backup options, alerts when website traffic spikes or your site goes down and tools for SEO analysis. At the time of this writing, a free account is available for managing up to five WordPress websites.

SWAIN LIBRARY: 19 THINGS FOR HAMDEN HALL

http://19things.wordpress.com/

One of the core principles in many a librarian's philosophy is to not simply give patrons an answer, but to teach them how to find the answer themselves. In today's society, this desire also extends to helping patrons with technology so they can share their work with others. At Swain Library in Connecticut, teachers come to the school librarian to learn how to create websites.

So far the librarian and faculty have collaborated to create seven websites using WordPress.com. Each website has its own theme and domain URL. Comments are turned on for most of the websites, as students are encouraged to participate in the online discussions. An example blog is 19 Things for Hamden Hall (as seen in the screen shot, fig. 14.3), which is based on the Learning 2.0 Project from the Public Library of Charlotte and Mecklenburg County.[9] The purpose of 19 Things was to introduce faculty to new technology and tools "in small bites."[10]

Sarah Ludwig, library department chair and academic technology coordinator at the Hamden Hall Country Day School in Connecticut, answered the survey about her library's usage of WordPress.

The Library and Its Users

Hamden Hall Country Day School is a private school located near Long Island Sound in southwestern Connecticut. The school is home to over 586 students from prekindergarten to the twelfth grade.[11] Students upon their graduation often enroll in very competitive colleges. Students enjoy a modern library with access to the Internet on school desktops and laptops, as well as wireless Internet.[12] Swain Library is located centrally on campus and is divided into two spaces: lower and upper. Preschoolers to sixth graders use the Lower School Library, while seventh to twelfth graders use the Upper School Library. Ludwig manages the older students' collection and another librarian takes care of the lower grades. Ludwig is also the department chair and so is responsible for the whole library.

FIGURE 14.3
Swain Library site

Why They Chose WordPress

The collaboration between Ludwig and the Hamden Hall faculty began because both sides need help in developing their own projects. For teachers, it was to learn how "to share information with our community about their classrooms and projects," while Lugwig writes that she wanted to kick off a "professional development program with faculty." Sometimes during a consultation, Ludwig will suggest a different platform to meet a teacher's needs. If students will need their own blogs,

Ludwig helps set up Edublogs accounts instead.[13] Otherwise, a very image-heavy blog may end up as a Tumblr.[14] Ludwig's experience with WordPress came from developing her own blog on the platform; she then started using it with teachers.

Building with WordPress

Since WordPress.com is free and domain names do not matter, setting up a new WordPress website is a quick affair. Ludwig notes that most websites take only a week or two to set up. When a teacher meets with Ludwig and it is decided that a blog would best suit their needs, they then work together to design the blog and customize the settings. For example, some blogs need a subscription button while another teacher wants to turn off the comments.

Starting a website is often a change of mindset for how the teachers think about their own work. They have concerns about publishing their writing for anyone to view. Ludwig tells the faculty, "It takes some getting used to, but eventually [you] will feel more comfortable." The next challenge is for the teacher to keep up the process of using the website on their own. While WordPress is easy to use, there is a process that has to be followed for each post. For example, to post a simple photo, you have to log in; open a new post; title it; upload the image; decide whether the image needs a title, caption, description, and so on; and how the image should appear on the page. While a blogger's work is rewarding when it is shared, it does take a time commitment, which can be a hurdle.

Websites are not backed up. Currently active blogs tend to be updated on a weekly basis. Older projects may be left in a frozen state as a testimony to a project that has been completed.

Evaluation

The websites are meeting the needs of the teachers. Regarding the 19 Things for Hamden Hall website, the blog saw 4,200 visitors and received 108 comments. Ludwig notes, "This was a big deal for our school!" Otherwise, Ludwig keeps track of site metrics by viewing the site analysis for each website. Some teachers have also undertaken the process of building their own WordPress websites without the librarian's help. However, these teachers may later ask Ludwig for advice in configuring comments and similar settings.

ADDITIONAL LIBRARIES

Berkhamsted School Library

http://berkschlibr.wordpress.com/

Located in southern England and run by four librarians, the BSH website is a book discussion blog. Each post includes cover images, links to more information, and the occasional video. Their website has many social sharing options, uses tags, and shows related articles.

Coleman Media Center

http://colemanmediacenter.org/

The front page of this site is dominated by a slideshow that comes from its premium Caliber theme.[15] The front page also boasts a Google calendar on agenda view, which makes it easy to see the library's upcoming events.

The Unquiet Library

http://theunquietlibrary.wordpress.com/

Images are large enough to take center stage on the Unquiet Library's website. The only thing that can overshadow the images is the attention to students' interests and issues. Videos of students explaining their work, slideshows, and frequent contests are announced through the site. The blog features several sidebar widgets for categories, a Flickr photostream, and more.

NOTES

1. DevPress, "Oxygen," http://theme.wordpress.com/themes/oxygen/.
2. Goodreads, www.goodreads.com/.
3. Escalante Valley Elementary School, http://escalantevalley.org/.
4. YOUmedia Chicago, http://youmediachicago.org/.
5. Wordle, www.wordle.net.
6. United States Geographical Survey, "Feature Detail Report for: Beryl," http://geonames.usgs.gov/pls/gnispublic/f?p=gnispq:3:61730333636184::NO::P3_FID:1437500.
7. "ManageWP," https://managewp.com/.

8. Solostream, "WP-DaVinci Premium WordPress Theme," www.solostream.com/wordpress-themes/wp-davinci/.

9. Charlotte Mecklenburg Library, "Learning 2.0: 23 Things," 2006, http://plcmcl2-things.blogspot.com/.

10. 19 Things from Hamden Hall, 2011, Swain Library, http://19things.wordpress.com/about/.

11. Hamden Hall Country Day School, "Quick Facts," www.hamdenhall.org/podium/default.aspx?t=126527.

12. Hamden Hall Country Day School, "Swain Library," www.hamdenhall.org/podium/default.aspx?t=126502.

13. Edublogs, http://edublogs.org/.

14. Tumblr, www.tumblr.com.

15. Theme Weaver, "Caliber," www.themeweaver.net/themes/caliber/.

Chapter Fifteen

Special Libraries and Allies

INTERNATIONAL CENTER OF PHOTOGRAPHY

http://icplibrary.wordpress.com/

The International Center of Photography (ICP) describes itself as "the world's leading institution dedicated to the understanding of photography in all its forms."[1] ICP offers classes and exhibitions, and provides researchers access to their collections. The ICP's library hosts its blog, *Monsters & Madonnas*, at WordPress .com. The blog's high-quality photos are the first draw to the site, but once you can stop examining the photos, you realize the images are merely a footnote on the page. It is the intense and thoughtful writing of the library staff that compels you to subscribe to the blog. Russet Lederman describes Takashi Homma's *Mushrooms from the Forest 2011* as "emotional, yet distant. We are left numb."[2] Simply typing here Lederman's comment on that book does not do justice to the emotional impact of her review in context, so I would suggest reading the post. This library blog differs from others in that not only does it belong to an institution's library, but each post is a wonderful read in and of itself.

The *Monsters & Madonnas* blog is unusual compared to other WordPress.com websites in this book because they have customized their Twenty Ten theme.[3] By paying the fee for the Custom Design upgrade, the library added a new background and title background to their website.[4] The simple upgrade allowed the library to make a website that has a similar feel to the ICP's main site, so the transition is less jarring. In addition, the title's background is very artistic, which works well for a photography blog, as seen in the screen shot (fig. 15.1).

FIGURE 15.1
International Center of Photography

The site has a simple interface. Aside from the full-width header and image, content is displayed in two columns. The left column is narrow and serves as the site's navigation. From top to bottom, there are widgets to search the website, an e-mail subscription button, a block highlighting an exhibit, archive links, a list of recent posts, a calendar, the categories, and finally imported Twitter tweets. In the main column are the posts themselves. The posts are not hidden behind Read More links but are shared in their lengthy glory. As you scroll down the website, more posts keep appearing—an effect known as an infinite scroll. There are no pages on the website. Each post has large, high-quality images to accompany the beautifully written text. Photos are displayed using a variety of WordPress gallery views. Clicking on an author's name takes you to their short biography and a list of their posts.

Deirdre Donohue, Stephanie Shuman Librarian at the International Center of Photography, answered the survey about her library's usage of WordPress.

The Library and Its Users

The patrons of the ICP Library all share a common passion: photography. When writing about her users, Donohue speaks of them as "folks using their first camera" to students both as teenagers and as serious international practitioners, as well as the ICP's own in-house team of faculty, staff, and curators. Another group is made of "scholars from throughout the world," Donohue writes. The ICP and its library are therefore a rich resource for the global photography community. The library's collection is accessible to the public only by appointment, but their mission "is to furnish information and inspiration to anyone interested in the medium," so they welcome all visitors.[5]

181

Why They Chose WordPress

The ICP Library holds an enviable position among libraries: their users are keenly interested in what the librarians are interested in. Donohue explains, "[The library's fans] asked to know what we liked and what new things we noticed." The site's content reflects the library's efforts to exceed their users' wishes. Development of the blog was a team effort at ICP. Approval for the blog was given by the deputy director for programs, who oversees the library. WordPress was not a new venture for the ICP; other branches of the institution are also using the software for their blogs. Additionally, ICP has a large community of alumni in over fifty countries and scholars from around the world "that want to stay connected as well," Donohue writes.

Building with WordPress

The library did not build the website but relied on the skills of ICP's Marketing and Communications Department. In particular, Donohue highlights the efforts of Sumy Cho as having done "the heavy lifting and worked with us to get what we wanted." Since the library saved money on not hiring an outsider to build the website, the only purchase required was for the ability to edit the theme and to buy larger media storage space. All this extra storage space is necessary for the high-quality images the blog uses.

Once the site was built, it was time for a test run. Staff added a few posts to test out their new platform. When that test was deemed successful, the library notified the internal e-mail list about their new site. Next, a link was added to the ICP's website. People began to take notice of the site and began to follow the posts. However, it was not until Donohue "started to Tweet the posts, the numbers got really healthy and we gained followers rapidly." The timeline from conception to deployment took only a month. The library continues to expand their stable of writers by encouraging interns and volunteers to post new content. Their involvement helps "because there are times of the year when none of the staff has time" to keep the site updated, Donohue explains. The site's valuable content is kept backed up via ICP's IT staff.

Evaluation

On the average day, the ICP Library sees around twenty-five patrons a day. However, their blog has over two hundred subscribers, which nets the library an outreach of additional two hundred to four hundred viewers per day, Donohue reports. She notes that sometimes a post will go viral and the blog will see four thousand visitors. This is an impressive feat for a very specialized institutional library! The real advantages have been drawing attention "to hidden collections and creating discussion around topics of great interest to our community," Donohue writes. Additionally, the blog has even led to new donations and received press coverage. These three side effects—finding a new audience, netting donations, and raising awareness—are incredible achievements for a hosted blog.

The site's statistics are monitored through WordPress's built-in tools. Donohue then gives these numbers to senior staff for further discussion. She notes that the blog has "exceeded everyone's expectations."

Special Features

Aside from the great blog title of *Monsters & Madonnas*, the ICL Library also has a great site design that harkens to the ICP's main website. In order to customize their Twenty Ten theme, the library had to purchase the Custom Design upgrade.[6]

The beautiful text on the blog is a special feature that is wholly dependent on the talents of the library's writers. However, anyone can capitalize on the idea to use images to make their WordPress website more attractive to visitors. The ICL Library supports the skill of student interns, who photograph and scan objects for the blog. A side benefit of the blog's photos is that each image is increasing the "internal digital assets" that the library holds, Donohue notes. (One way to produce better-looking photos is to take well-lit photos. At my library, we purchased a photo light box.[7] I use it as a way to light objects when I am filming a video tutorial. The increase in quality has been immense, as the old videos were dingy and yellow using just the library's overhead light.)

LANIER THEOLOGICAL LIBRARY

www.laniertheologicallibrary.org

Attention to detail is a specialty of the Lanier Theological Library (LTL). An online video tour of the library gives the curious a glimpse of the inside of this impressive building and the collections within.[8] Therefore the website that connects the theology community to the library needs to be just as impressive and usable. For their online venture, the library chose WordPress as their platform. Features of the website include image sliders, embedded videos, and online registration for events.

The website is a customized version of the Latitude theme built on the Genesis Framework.[9] The header includes a full-width title with the Lanier logo. The menu is presented as a horizontal navigation scheme with drop-down menus when a menu item is hovered over. Each major section of the website has the appearance of a tabbed menu, as the background of that section's link is the same white as the background of the website. The home page enlists a page-width image slider of the latest stories, as seen in the screen shot (fig. 15.2). Below the slider is a three-column grid of different areas of interest on the website. A mailing list form is also present. A second image slider is found lower on the page featuring photos of the library. In the website's footer is the contact information, social media links, and a note that the library foundation is a Texas non-profit corporation. Meta information is below the top footer, which includes information about the WordPress site and a log-in link. Other page layouts alternate between a two-column design with the sidebar to the left and a three-column design that has sidebars flanking either side of the main content area. The left sidebar is a secondary menu for that section

FIGURE 15.2
Lanier Theological Library

of the website. On the right, information about upcoming events, links to other prominent areas of the website, and social media links are present.

Amy Parker, former assistant, and Emily Brown, current assistant at the Lanier Theological Library in Texas, answered the survey about their library's usage of WordPress.

The Library and Its Users

The LTL is located on the northwestern side of Houston, Texas. The library is the vision of lawyer Mark Lanier. He has served as a Sunday school teacher. His lessons were well documented with footnotes based on primary resources. He decided to share his love of books and theology by constructing the LTL in 2010.[10] The library's collections include works on "linguistics, church history, Egyptology, the Dead Sea Scrolls and theology in general."[11] Other areas of interest are display pieces and a lecture series. Usage of the library's materials is free and open to the public, although no books may leave the building.

The library's users are made up of two distinct groups: scholar/researchers and nonacademic visitors. Scholars travel a distance to use the library's growing collection in their research. Most of the one thousand patrons are religious scholars, including "pastors who come in to prepare their sermons," Brown writes. Parker notes that nonscholars are interested in the building and come to just see the collection.

Why They Chose WordPress

Parker was not present when the decision was made to use WordPress for the library's website. She writes that an outside firm originally built the website in WordPress. After Parker began to review the resulting website and got to know WordPress, she realized that the website was not meeting the needs of their patrons. At first, she sent instructions to the firm to redesign the site to her specifications. Since then she has learned WordPress herself and launched the redesigned website in August 2012.

The library chose WordPress because it could be used to set up the website just the way the library wanted it to be done, could be easily themed, and was easy to manage. Parker notes that the website needs to be a "business card" for the library itself. As such, the library's website needed to meet these goals, she writes:

- Define what the library is and who it's for
- Explain how to use the library
- Spread information about the library's upcoming events
- Explain how to use our online resources such as the online catalog and journals databases
- Give the library's backstory
- Establish the library's "branding"

WordPress has allowed the library to meet and surpass these goals.

Building with WordPress

Once Parker started to work on the library's website herself, she set to work on researching other libraries' websites. She made note of features that she felt worked best to suit the needs of her patrons that she "wanted to imitate." As she worked on the website, she was able to delve into the numerous tutorials and support forums that are available thanks to the WordPress community.

Finding the right layout and navigational scheme was a challenge for Parker. Scholars need a website that will provide them with ways to understand and access the collection before visiting. For nonacademics, the website needs to be accessible for nonexperts. Parker designed the website to reconcile these two audiences. For example, the site's home page is broken into categories to introduce a new person to the library as well providing an introduction for starting research at the facility. Links use concise but natural language to direct the web visitor on how to use the library. One of the primary links is titled "Using the Library," which breaks down how the library works.

The library needed a theme that Parker could use to build a powerful website even as a novice. She chose the Genesis framework because "it had a user-friendly yet customizable set up." To modify the Latitude theme, she created a child theme to keep her site's unique code from being altered whenever the Latitude theme needed to be updated. As Parker familiarized herself with WordPress, she writes that "it was perfect for a beginner and now, I'm still intrigued by the system and the process of trying to implement new elements or plugins on the site."

Evaluation

Since there was a personnel change at the library during the writing this book, information about how the site is doing was unavailable. Brown writes that their website is monitored and analyzed by a team, but she is still learning about the website.

Special Features

The LTL website relies on the Genesis framework and Latitude theme to empower their website. However, a mix of plugins helped to customize the website for the library's unique needs. The home page uses the SlideDeck 2 Lite Responsive

Content Slider.[12] Content can be easily added to the slider through an easy-to-use interface. Content can be pulled in from other social sharing services such as YouTube and Flickr. A highlight of this slider is that in the top right corner of all slides is a sharing interface. Site visitors can click on this button to instantly share the Slidedeck on their own social networks. A number of different themes for the SlideDeck are also available, but the full range is available only by upgrading to the premium version of the plugin.

Site visitors can join the mailing list from the homepage. The MailChimp List Subscribe Form plugin adds a widget to the LTL website.[13] This widget captures the subscriber's name and e-mail address and allows them to choose which mailing lists to join. MailChimp offers both free and paid e-mail newsletter subscriptions, so if you use this service, the plugin is ideal to maximize your mailing list outreach.[14]

Since an integral part of the LTL is their event series, it is vital that the events are displayed in a meaningful way on their website. For this purpose, the library uses the Events Calendar plugin.[15] The LTL displays events using the List View, which displays event information in two columns. The left column displays the event's date, title, and description. The right column gives more detailed information about the date and time, location, and cost. Premium features are also available that allow you to sell tickets, send information to Facebook, and more.

LEARN@THE CORKBOARD

http://learn.thecorkboard.org/

Learning management systems (LMS) such as Blackboard or Moodle are purchased by universities to add an online component to in-person classes or serve as the sole classroom for distance learning students. These LMS are costly—even open source forms require support services—and usually cookie-cutter in appearance. They also link across all classes regardless of whether the teacher decides to use all the built-in functionalities. At the innovative University of Wisconsin–Madison's School of Library and Information Studies, one doctoral student built his own WordPress website that he uses while teaching his students. The website uses WordPress's social platform, BuddyPress, to make the student community interactive.

Learn@The Corkboard is a subdomain of the instructor's personal website, the Corkboard.[16] Therefore both sites share a similar visual appearance and arrangement of content. The design— a soft blue patterned background—is not

FIGURE 15.3
Learn@The Corkboard

intrusive or distracting, which is vital for a learning environment. Navigation is to the top right using drop-down menus, as seen in the screen shot (fig. 15.3). Some of the links go offsite; for example, to the Madison Libraries' course reserves page. Other links include information about the course, features unique to the

LMS (e.g., the forums and badge system), and a link to a variety of RSS feeds for the website. The main content on the front page displays the avatars of which students are online and includes a list of recent activity by the students. These features serve to show which students are around to chat with about assignments and keeps the site focused on student work. Student profiles list information about their achievements, friends, and their recent activity on the website. In the footer is a simple calendar, a drop-down menu for the site's archives, a list of groups, and a display of recently active members.

Kyle M. L. Jones, doctoral student at the University of Wisconsin–Madison School of Library and Information Studies, answered the survey about his library school course's usage of WordPress.

Note: Jones is a coauthor of two books about the use of WordPress in libraries. His website is a demonstration of him practicing what he preaches!

The Library and Its Users

The University of Wisconsin–Madison's School of Library and Information Studies is located in southern Wisconsin.[17] The department consists of appropriately 225 students, faculty, and staff members.[18] Jones teaches twelve students per course who have a wide range of technical skills. His website was used for his summer 2012 class, Digital Tools, Trends and Debates.

Why They Chose WordPress

In his student and working life, Jones has come to understand the limitations of a traditional LMS platform. He notes that these LMSs force a closed system on the instructor and students, which prevents a wider conversation with the library profession at large. His goal throughout his class was to "[engage] my students with the professionals in the field of library and information studies (LIS)" with a publicly accessible online classroom. As a consultant, Jones had previous experience building online learning environments with WordPress. Using his skills and knowledge, he was well qualified to evaluate WordPress and tweak it to suit his needs as an instructor. His students, judging by evidence of the summer 2012 course's activity stream, were thoroughly engaged with the platform. Jones has also worked with the open source platforms Drupal and Moodle, but his professional work with WordPress afforded him the skills to adapt the platform as needed.

Building with WordPress

Because Jones maintains an active website for himself, he did not need to purchase additional resources for his online course. The only new thing he acquired was the website's subdomain. Jones was able to build a working prototype of the website within a month, which was his first milestone. With such a quick development time, he was able to modify the website at his leisure for a few months as he thought of new improvements. Then he completely rebuilt the site within a few days. He keeps the site's plugins updated thanks to experience (his previous WordPress websites have been hacked before). He does his own backups and site maintenance. However, he would like to "offload the hosting and backups to someone else, like my institution's instructional technology department."

While it was easy to see student involvement through the class's activity stream, Jones needed a way to see the work the students were doing. Therefore, all assignments were submitted as blog posts to the website. Jones then checked his students' work twice a day. He could see when students had added their assignments by looking for new posts on their blogs. In his RSS reader, Jones had subscribed to his students' RSS feeds for each blog. His mechanisms for tracking and grading their work were done separately outside of WordPress.

Evaluation

Jones was able to use WordPress as a learning environment to help teach his students the course objectives about web technology and LIS issues. He writes that WordPress taught his students about blogging, about the social aspects of online collaborative learning such as forums and activity updates, and about the ramifications of posting content online. His students were confronted with these "socio-technical issues" about their privacy and whether they have ownership over their own content, Jones writes. His class was successful, and feedback was actively solicited about the learning environment throughout the course. Additionally, his students were asked for qualitative information about their experiences using the WordPress site when they reviewed the class. Jones also integrated Google Analytics into his website to track student usage of the site.

Special Features

Jones purchased the premium WordPress theme, Kaboodle from WOO Themes, for the Corkboard.[19] He notes that the theme had to be modified to work with

BuddyPress. This theme has some built-in ability to customize the appearance through alternative color schemes and background images. Kaboodle is targeted toward portfolio-style websites, but as Jones shows, the theme can be customized to work beautifully for an LMS. He states that "an undervalued part of online learning is the aesthetic experience (see the generally awful designs of traditional LMSs) and I wanted my students to enjoy seeing as well as experiencing the course site." His students' enthusiastic usage and evaluation of the site is a testimony to his good judgment.

Jones points out that his class website lacks traditional LMS features. His site has "no quizzes, no gradebooks, etc." A few plugins have been developed for teachers to fill the LMS gap in WordPress. One is BuddyPress Courseware which creates a class dashboard, a gradebook, quizzes, a calendar, and more.[20] Learninglog is marketed toward teachers with younger students.[21] The teacher sets up a learning log that individual or groups of students can work on together, which makes it easy for the teacher to see the submissions. The CP Appointment Calendar plugin could be useful for allowing students to schedule meetings with you.[22] Then the Smallerik File Browser plugin could allow students to "access their own repository where to upload homework and download corrections or other personal files."[23] Finally, WP Teacher creates new content types of Assignments and Events that allow the teacher to put together a quick site listing assignment dates and that allow students to upload their assignments.[24] A combination of free plugins and clever implementations can help you build a LMS style website for your library-led classes, or even for teachers.

191

WEBSITE IN A BOX

http://utahlibraries.org/website/

Aside from teaching patrons or teachers how to use WordPress, a library can dig deeper and teach other libraries how to build their own websites. Colleen B. Eggett discovered by doing an environmental scan that 26 percent of public libraries in Utah had no website of their own. Does it hinder a library to not have a website? What is the role of a library's website in their work? These questions were posed on a LinkedIn discussion board for International Federation of Library Associations and Institutions (IFLA) members recently. Emad E. Saleh, an LIS professor from Saudi Arabia, summarized that a library's website is an access point; it raises awareness of the library and its role; "[meets] library users wherever they are"; and serves as a tool for connecting to potential new users.[25] For over a quarter of

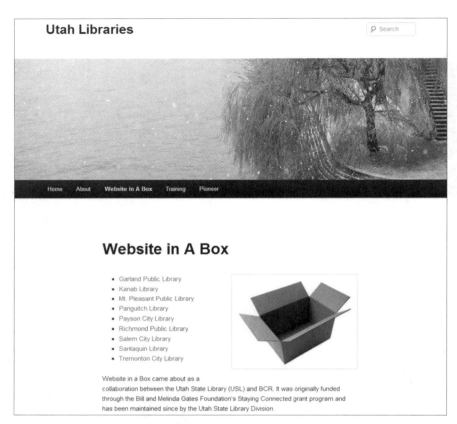

FIGURE 15.4
Website in a Box

public libraries in Utah not to have an online presence puts them at a disadvantage not only locally, but also against big search engines such as Google. Similarly, for many people, if you are not online, you may as well not exist. So, the Utah State Library (USL) set up the Website in a Box project to help libraries get themselves online (fig. 15.4).

Because the project's goal is to teach other libraries to build a website of their own, there is no single website to describe. The project's website uses a default installation of Twenty Eleven. Each public library's website uses their own theme, which they may or may not have customized further. The site in the screen shot is the home page of the WIAB project.

Colleen B. Eggett, training coordinator/consultant at Utah State Library in Salt Lake City, Utah, answered the survey about her library's usage of WordPress.

The Library and Its Users

When Eggett realized how many public libraries in Utah lacked their own website, she and the Utah State Library took action to help libraries. For the Website in a Box (WIAB) project, library directors were invited to come to a workshop to build a WordPress website. The library directors were between 30 and 60 years of age, mostly falling into the range of 40 to 50 years old. Some of the attendees were staff that the directors had brought with them. Each library represented had a population under 25,000 people, and each had Internet access available at their library.

The participants were enthusiastic to build a website to better serve their communities, but they also had a range of challenges. The first was their comfort level with technology. Some people felt at home dabbling with websites while others had just a passing familiarity with computers. Eggett sums up the participants as being "committed, excited, timid, technically challenged, [and] desirous of making a difference in their community." Attendees were also worried that they would break their websites—which, Eggett points out, "they sometimes did!" Finally, the libraries did not have the resources in place to build a website on their own. The WIAB project thus fulfilled a vital need for these institutions.

It should be noted that the WIAB project had a competitive selection process for which libraries could participate. The participants were selected by a panel of USL judges based on their applications. Eggett writes that the applicants had to show:

- They would maintain a website.
- A website met the needs of their community.
- They could not build a website through other means.

Once the libraries were selected, they were invited to the workshop to begin building their website.

Why They Chose WordPress

The WIAB was a collaborative effort between the USL and the Bibliographical Center for Research (BCR; the BCR has since been acquired by Lyrasis). Egget of the USL took care of the planning, funding, promotional, and project management decisions. Meanwhile, Shelly Drum, the technology training coordinator at BCR, worked on the technical decisions, which included the initial setups for the websites. According to Eggett, others who were involved in this joint project included Craig Neilson, library resources program manager, and Donna Jones

Morris, state librarian, of the Utah State Library; and Regan Harper, BCR's director of training and services.

The USL and BCR knew that they wanted a blogging platform for these new websites. They reviewed Blogger and other blogging platforms before settling on WordPress. The features that appealed to the collaborators were the social interactivity of blogging (e.g., comments, sharing), the ease of usage, and of course the low, low price of being free to use. The WIAB project could not be built on a platform that required annual fees for usage, Eggett notes. When they did a thorough review of WordPress in professional literature, it was shown that the software was reliable and well received.

Building with WordPress

The total time of putting the WIAB together was six months. This process included developing the project, organizing training, and seeking approval of all parties. Funding came originally from a Bill and Melinda Gates Staying Connected grant, then later from state money through Utah State Library.[26] Chosen participants had their mileage and meals paid for through the grant. Later, when their websites went live, the grant money paid for three years of hosting and domain purchases.

Creating multiple new websites meant obtaining new resources for the WIAB project. First, domain URLs and hosting space were purchased. USL then hired Drum to set up the websites, design a theme template, train the libraries, and provide technical support for three years. These support sessions met in-person every few months. Participants were also given training manuals in print and on a CD so "that a variety of learning styles [could] be met," Eggett writes. At the start of the project, there was a meeting at two different locations so participants could meet one another. For three libraries that could not journey to the meeting, Eggett went to them to get them started.

Libraries with Drumm's support designed their own sites. Each initial site looked alike, but then the libraries chose their own themes. Some participants decided to ditch the blog style; others chose their colors based on their local town's website. Each site evolved over time to look very different from the original template. However, all websites have to meet USL's certification process. These requirements include—and are general good practices for library websites—the library's hours, contact and library program information, and a link to the Pioneer: Utah's Online Library, Eggett writes. Libraries sent more advanced design requests in and then the developer turned her hours over to get paid for this time.

Evaluation

After three years, all the libraries are self-sufficient in maintaining their own websites. When a library runs into trouble, they can call Eggett for technical assistance. Eggett was originally the idea and program planner for WIAB, but she has become very well acquainted with WordPress since then. A few of the sites have also gone offline because the hosting library did not have the resources or their town incorporated the library into the town's website.

Site statistic–wise, Eggett reports that the WIAB websites have received "hundreds and thousands of hits." In the first six months, one site achieved over 100,000 hits, while another library's town was so impressed that the local city government also built themselves a website. Eggett writes that "[this] project turned out to be very meaningful to the libraries and the communities that participated."

ADDITIONAL LIBRARIES

McIntosch Memorial Library

www.mmlibrary.org

The distinguishing feature of this website is that it uses WordPress as a catalog. On the catalog page, each section is represented by a button (e.g., Picture Books). Clicking on a section takes you to a page listing all the books under that section header. Books have call numbers and are tagged by topic. Each section of the catalog has a two-column display. Videos for how this site was built can be viewed at the Build Your Own Business Website's case study page.[27]

NOTES

1. International Center of Photography, "About ICP," 2011, www.icp.org/about-icp.

2. *Monsters & Madonnas,* "Hidden Dangers: Japanese Photobooks in the Shadow of Fukushima," 2012, http://icplibrary.wordpress.com/2012/10/23/hidden-dangers-fukushima/.

3. WordPress.com, "Twenty Ten," http://theme.wordpress.com/themes/twentyten/.

4. WordPress.com, "Custom Design," http://en.support.wordpress.com/custom-design/.

5. International Center of Photography, "Library," www.icp.org/research-center/library.

6. WordPress.com, "Custom Design."

7. In particular, the Adorama De-Shadow Box, www.adorama.com/VRDSB1616.html?gclid=COHfv-nzs7MCFcRa4Aod8GgA7g

8. Mark Lanier, "The Lanier Library and Stone Chapel (HD version)," video, 2:59, 2012, http://vimeo.com/30457007.

9. ThemePix, "Latitude," http://themepix.com/wordpress-themes/latitude/preview/; StudioPress, "The Genesis Framework," www.studiopress.com/.

10. "Bibliophile Mark Lanier Builds a Theological Library," *The Super Lawyers Blog*, March 8, 2011, http://blog.superlawyers.com/2011/03/articles-1/news-and-iformation/bibliophile-mark-lanier-builds-a-theological-library.

11. Diane Cowen, "Lanier Shares Love of Theology through New Library, Speaker Series," Chron, March 3, 2011, www.chron.com/life/houston-belief/article/Lanier-shares-love-of-theology-through-new-1687721.php#photo-1215046.

12. dtelepathy et al., "SlideDeck 2 Lite Responsive Content Slider," http://wordpress.org/extend/plugins/slidedeck2/.

13. mc_jesse and crowdfavorite, "MailChimp List Subscribe Form," http://wordpress.org/extend/plugins/mailchimp/.

14. MailChimp, http://mailchimp.com/.

15. ModernTribe et al., "The Events Calendar," http://wordpress.org/extend/plugins/the-events-calendar/.

16. The Corkboard, http://thecorkboard.org/.

17. University of Wisconsin–Madison, "School of Library & Information Studies," www.slis.wisc.edu/index.htm.

18. University of Wisconsin–Madison, "School of Library & Information Studies: About," www.slis.wisc.edu/about.htm.

19. WOO Themes, "Kaboodle," www.woothemes.com/products/kaboodle/.

20. Stas Suşcov et al., "BuddyPress Courseware," http://wordpress.org/extend/plugins/buddypress-courseware/.

21. Tom and Andrea Cantieni, "Learninglog," http://wordpress.org/extend/plugins/learninglog/.

22. Codepeople, "CP Appointment Calendar," http://wordpress.org/extend/plugins/cp-appointment-calendar/.

23. smallerik, "Smallerik File Browser," http://wordpress.org/extend/plugins/smallerik-file-browser/.

24. Fredlawl and brysem, "WP Teacher," http://wordpress.org/extend/plugins/wp-teacher/.

25. Emad E. Saleh, comment on a LinkedIn discussion to the post "The Role of Library Websites: Your Experience," 2012, www.linkedin.com/groups/Role-Library-Websites-your-experience-796937.S.145355942.

26. Bill and Melinda Gates Foundation, www.gatesfoundation.org; Utah State Library, http://utahlibraries.org/website/.

27. "Community Library Website," Build Your Own Business, last accessed January 3, 2013, www.byobwebsite.com/case-studies/community-library-website/.

The Survey

1. Please describe your library.
2. What is your service population like?

    e.g., age range of users, tech savviness of community, home and/or mobile Internet access, etc.

3. What was the perceived need that your website was built to meet and how did you arrive at that conclusion?

    e.g., market research, other libraries have this, etc.

4. Who was involved in the decision making process for this website?
5. Why did your library choose WordPress over other platforms?
6. How was the website implemented?

    e.g., in-house, hired a designer, or both or other

7. What new resources did you have to obtain for this website?

    e.g., server, domain name, new staff person, etc.

8. What was the length of time from deciding a website was needed till the website launched?
9. What were the major milestones?

    e.g., did user testing, hired a web designer, etc.

10. How is the site being maintained (e.g. creating the content, updating the plugins, etc.) and is it being backed up?
11. How well is the website meeting the needs of your patrons and your library's goals?
12. Referring to your answer to the previous question, what assessment methods are you using to evaluate the website?

13. Please briefly describe how you created those features of your website that I highlighted in my e-mail to you.

    e.g., plugins, programmers, etc.

14. Do you have any interesting statistics or results that you may share related to your website?

Resources for WordPress

For Libraries

Dodson, Joshua. "WordPress as a Content Management System for a Library Web Site: How to Create a Dynamically Generated Subject Guide." *Code4Lib Journal* 3 (2008). http://journal.code4lib.org/articles/76.

Dodson lists his process, shares bits of code, and shows screen shots of how he developed subject guides in WordPress.

Farrington, Polly-Alida, and Kyle M. L. Jones. *ALA Library Technology Report on WordPress for Libraries*. Chicago: ALA Editions, 2011.

This book offers a brief background on WordPress, then makes suggestions for possible further development of WordPress. It covers how to install WordPress and set it up, lists recommended library-related plugins, and ends with guest pieces. These guest writers discuss everything from how WordPress can help with the user experience to how to create subject guides. As a Library Technology Report, this book comes in at sixty pages, so each section is very brief.

Farrington, Polly-Alida, and Kyle M. L. Jones. *Learning from Libraries that Use WordPress: Content Management Systems Best Practices and Case Studies*. Chicago: American Library Association, 2012.

This book is the extended version of the previous title, with further guest pieces and a cookbook section with recipes, such as creating a better workflow or rolling out your own social network.

WordPress and Librarians. https://www.facebook.com/groups/wordpress.librarians.

Want to chat with other librarians about WordPress? Then join this growing community of hundreds of librarians! Members typically post questions, share helpful information, and showcase their new WordPress websites.

WordPress Libraries Examples. http://lib20.pbworks.com/w/page/59677899/WordPress-Libraries-examples.

Polly-Alida Farrington has created this list of libraries using WordPress grouped together by type of library.

General WordPress Resources

Books

Casabona, Joe. *Building WordPress Themes from Scratch*. Rockable Press, 2012.

Learn how to build your own WordPress themes with this colorful book, which includes code snippets and specific instructions on how to code your theme.

Majure, Janet. *Teach Yourself Visually WordPress*. 2nd ed. Indianapolis: John Wiley & Sons, 2012.

Use this visual step-by-step guide to set up your WordPress website. Majure includes large images, clear instructions, and even highlights questions you may have—and then provides solid answers.

Websites

Andrew, Paul. "20 Snippets and Hacks to Make WordPress User-Friendly for Your Clients." April 27, 2011. http://speckyboy.com/2011/04/27/20-snippets-and-hacks-to-make-wordpress-user-friendly-for-your-clients/2011.

These snippets simplify the interface for your users by removing unnecessary boxes and columns, and customizing the dashboard.

Gordon, Zac. "Getting Started with WordPress Multisite." http://blog.teamtreehouse.com/getting-started-with-wordpress-multisite.

While Multisite is now baked into WordPress, you still need to activate it. Gordon also points to further resources and gives you tips on managing a multisite.

Hansen, David. "Advanced Layout Templates in WordPress' Content Editor." October 14, 2011. http://wp.smashingmagazine.com/2011/10/14/advanced-layout-templates-in-wordpress-content-editor/.

Learn how to lay out columns within WordPress's content editor.

Kouratoras, Konstantinos. "WordPress Shortcodes: A Complete Guide." May 1, 2012. http://wp.smashingmagazine.com/2012/05/01/wordpress-shortcodes -complete-guide/.

This article offers basic and advanced shortcode techniques and even how to add shortcodes to widgets.

Leary, Kevin. "WordPress Multisite: Practical Functions and Methods." November 17, 2011. http://wp.smashingmagazine.com/2011/11/17/ wordpress-multisite-practical-functions-methods/.

Hosting a multisite? Pull out useful content to share from the network with these helpful tips.

Pataki, Daniel. "The Complete Guide to Custom Post Types." November 8, 2012. http://wp.smashingmagazine.com/2012/11/08/complete-guide-custom-post -types/.

This guide gives you the example of creating a product custom post type, taxonomy, and post meta boxes.

Patterson, Hugh III. "OAI-PMH for WordPress." March 6, 2012. http://hugh .thejourneyler.org/2012/oai-pmh-for-wordpress/.

Patterson gives an overview of how OAI-PMH services could be created in WordPress.

Rice, Nathan. "Creating a Blog Page – With Paging." www.wpbeginner.com/ wp-tutorials/how-to-create-a-separate-page-for-blog-posts-in-wordpress/.

Rice offers three methods to create your page of posts.

Shepherd, Richard. "Create Your First WordPress Custom Post Type." August 7, 2012. http://blog.teamtreehouse.com/create-your-first-wordpress-custom -post-type.

This guide walks you through the steps of creating a portfolio custom post type.

WordPress.org. "Codex." http://codex.wordpress.org/.

The online manual for WordPress is written at an intermediate level. You may need to ask for help to understand the codex if you are new to coding.

WordPress.org. "Shortcodes API." http://codex.wordpress.org/Shortcode_API.

For advanced users, the official documentation on shortcodes is very detailed.

Web Developer Resources

All the titles in the A Book Apart (www.abookapart.com) series are great resources for web developers. These books are aimed at the busy professional, so each book is as short as possible while packing in loads of information. For the newcomer to web design and site building, the books may be beyond your depth. However, the language is simple, and sufficient resources and examples are provided so that with a little fortitude, you will obtain a thorough introduction on the subject matter.

Accessibility

Juicy Studio. "Luminosity Colour Contrast Ratio Analyser." http://juicystudio
.com/services/luminositycontrastratio.php.

   Check to see if your foreground and background colors have a high level of contrast. If the contrast is too weak, your users may have difficult using your website.

The Nemours Foundation. "What It's Like to be Color Blind." http://kidshealth
.org/kid/talk/qa/color_blind.html.

   Watch a short video about how colors appear to someone who is colorblind and how he compensates for it. The video is geared toward children but gives a great introduction to the topic.

United States Access Board. "Section 508 Homepage: Electronic and Information Technology." www.access-board.gov/508.htm.

   Learn about the latest Section 508 requirements straight from the federal government. The Web-based Intranet and Internet Information Applications section gives very specific examples of how to implement the requirements (www.access-board.gov/sec508/guide/1194.22.htm).

Web Accessibility in Mind. "Web Accessibility Evaluation Tool." http://wave
.webaim.org/.

   Enter your site's address, upload a file, or paste your code to see how your site is falling short of being accessible to all your visitors.

World Wide Web Consortium. "Web Accessibility Initiative (WAI)."
www.w3.org/WAI/.

   The W3C is responsible for the development and improvement of the Internet. Their website lists the worldwide developments in web accessibility. You can find a wide range of materials on how to plan for accessibility and how to evaluate your work, as well as tutorials for viewing.

General

Lynch, Patrick J., and Sarah Horton. *Web Style Guide.*, 3rd ed.. New Haven, CT: Yale University Press, 2008.

A few years old now, this book is a more in-depth look at the topics we covered in the "Website Planning" section. The book covers usability, information architecture, site structure, page structure, and more.

Layouts

Awwwards Team. "Grid Based Web Design Resources." www.awwwards.com/grid-based-web-design-resources.html.

Awwwards has developed a resource of tools, frameworks, templates, and more to get you started on grid systems.

Carusone, Antonio. "The Grid System." www.thegridsystem.org/.

This website collects information about grid systems via articles, templates, blogs, and more.

Hamilton, Stephanie. "The Concept of Balance in Web Design." August 25, 2011. www.onextrapixel.com/2011/08/25/concept-and-factors-of-balance-in-web-design/.

A great introduction to balanced web design with clear visuals and explanations.

Muller-Brockmann, J. *Grid Systems in Graphic Design.* Sulgen, Switzerland: Verlag Niggli AG, 1996.

Muller-Brockmann's book has been reprinted several times since the first publication in 1966. This book is a visual go-to bible for understanding how to layout designs on a grid.

Security

Baker, Rachel, Brad Williams, and John Ford. "Locking Down WordPress." July 10, 2012. http://build.codepoet.com/2012/07/10/locking-down-wordpress/.

This book is freely available online in different formats. It is provided by the Automattic, the parent company of WordPress. Make sure to check out the other resources on the website, as this is a rich resource for all things WordPress!

Derkin, Blue. "10 Ways to Beef Up Your Website's Security." June 15, 2010. www.smashingmagazine.com/2010/06/15/10-ways-to-beef-up-your-websites-security/.

While many of these tips from *Smashing Magazine* are common sense (e.g., your password should not be "password"!), other suggestions may cause you to rethink shared web hosting, for example.

WordPress.org. "Hardening WordPress." http://codex.wordpress.org/Hardening_WordPress.

The WordPress Codex describes various ways that your website may be compromised and then offers solutions to protect your website.

Style Guides

Cox, Patrick. "Do I Really Need a Style Guide?" September 6, 2012. http://tympanus.net/codrops/2012/09/06/do-i-really-need-a-style-guide/.

Cox answers your questions about if and when you need a style guide for your web project. Then he links to guides from big-brand companies like Apple and Cisco.

Neville, Kat. "Designing Style Guidelines for Brands and Websites." July 21, 2010. www.smashingmagazine.com/2010/07/21/designing-style-guidelines-for-brands-and-websites/.

Neville offers tips on what to include in your style guide. Highlights include how to handle logos, colors, white space, layouts, coding standards, format rules, and more.

Quinn, Amy. "Creating Successful Style Guides." February 15, 2010. http://johnnyholland.org/2010/02/creating-successful-style-guides/.

Light on images, this article from the Johnny Holland website sets you up with the mind-set for what to think about while creating your style guides.

User Experience

Allen, Jesmond, and James Chudley. *Smashing UX Design: Foundations for Designing Online User Experiences.* West Sussex, UK: John Wiley & Sons, 2012.

You know you need to build your website so that is usable for your patrons. Allen and Chudley give a brief introduction on the importance of UX. They then describe how to learn about the project you have been hired to do and give a detailed breakdown of all the different ways you can solicit feedback and test a website.

Foraker Labs. "Usability First." www.usabilityfirst.com.

Read articles about usability and user-centered design methodology. An added bonus is the glossary on usability terms, which also includes a list of related terms for each word.

"Information Architecture Library." The Information Architecture Institute. http://iainstitute.org/library/.

Learn from the experts about how to develop your website's IA to the best standards.

Krug, Steve. *Don't Make Me Think: A Common Sense Approach to Web Usability*. Berkeley, CA: New Riders, 2006.

The most basic website usability bible that will teach you how to think about your website visitors.

Plugins

Contact Forms

cforms

www.deliciousdays.com/cforms-plugin/

A completely customizable form creation plugin. This plugin was used on The Grove's website.

Contact Form 7

http://wordpress.org/extend/plugins/contact-form-7/

Let your users send you direct feedback without opening their own e-mail client. This plugin was used on the Teen Summer Challenge website.

Gravity Forms

www.gravityforms.com

If a simple contact form won't cut it, check out this paid form creation plugin. This plugin was used on the Topeka & Shawnee County Public Library website.

MailChimp List Subscribe Form

http://wordpress.org/extend/plugins/mailchimp/

Allow users to add themselves to your MailChimp mailing list using this widget based plugin. This plugin was used on the Lanier Theological Library website.

Content Management

Anthologize

http://wordpress.org/extend/plugins/anthologize/

Need a publishing platform? The Anthologize plugin exports your posts in several book formats including PFF, EPUB, and TEI.

Broken Link Checker

http://wordpress.org/extend/plugins/broken-link-checker/

Checking for broken links is a time-consuming process. This plugin produces a report and lets you edit the links from one screen, which saves you time.

Custom Post Type UI

http://wordpress.org/extend/plugins/custom-post-type-ui/

Quickly create custom post types and taxonomies. This plugin gives you several options to choose from regarding how your custom post type will interact and display on your website.

CSV Importer

http://wordpress.org/extend/plugins/csv-importer/

If you prefer to keep your data in spreadsheets before uploading them to your website, this plugin will bulk create posts for you from your CVS file. Make sure to set the correct headings to match the plugins settings before importing.

Dublin Core Metadata

http://wordpress.org/extend/plugins/dublin-core-metadata/

If you are creating a digital library of materials, you can automatically add custom Dublin Core fields to your posts. This plugin standardizes your resources so that no entry is missing a field.

Edit Flow

http://wordpress.org/extend/plugins/edit-flow/

Add an editorial calendar to your website, create your own workflow status labels, receive updates on the workflow, and more. The plugin is very well documented.

The Events Calendar

http://wordpress.org/extend/plugins/the-events-calendar/

Create a modern and professional calendar system using this free plugin. Additional features can be added by purchasing the premium version. This plugin was used on the Lanier Theological Library website.

PostMash Custom

http://wordpress.org/extend/plugins/postmash-custom/

Reorder pages in your menus using this drag-and-drop interface plugin. It is a resource hog, so disable it after use.

Pages Posts

http://wordpress.org/extend/plugins/pages-posts/

Create pages of posts quickly by configuring which plugin or page to show per page.

Post Expirator

http://wordpress.org/extend/plugins/post-expirator/

Stop manually changing your content from published to unpublished! This plugin adds a widget to your sidebar content that you configure during content creation so the content will unpublish itself or move to a new category.

Scripto

http://wordpress.org/extend/plugins/groupdocs-documents-annotation/

Are you uploading a lot of handwritten documents to your website? Harness the power of your community with this transcription tool, which is also available for Omeka and Drupal websites.

Types

http://wordpress.org/extend/plugins/types/

A great plugin that allows you to define custom post types, taxonomies, and fields. The list of supported fields include check boxes, radio buttons, image uploads, and more. The interface is user friendly.

WP Document Revisions

http://wordpress.org/extend/plugins/wp-document-revisions/

Use WordPress as a document revision repository and for document sharing. Upload documents to WordPress, then make a revision note and stop others from working on the same document at the same time.

209

WP SIMILE Timeline

http://wordpress.org/extend/plugins/wp-simile-timeline/

Create timelines for your digital collections based on your WordPress categories. Each timeline is embedded within a page.

Zotpress

http://wordpress.org/extend/plugins/zotpress/

Cite your sources using this plugin, which displays your Zotero citations. Users can download your citation list as well.

Dashboard

WP Total Hacks

http://wordpress.org/extend/plugins/wp-total-hacks/

Customizes your WordPress's administer logo, edits the dashboard footer, removes dashboard widget boxes, and more.

Erident Custom Login and Dashboard

http://wordpress.org/extend/plugins/erident-custom-login-and-dashboard/

Customizes the log-in screen and the dashboard's footer.

Simple History

http://wordpress.org/extend/plugins/simple-history/

See who has added or changed content on your website right from your dashboard.

Dashboard Notepad

http://wordpress.org/extend/plugins/dashboard-notepad/

Instead of sending an e-mail, leave a dashboard note for users of certain roles.

Design

Enhanced Text Widget

http://wordpress.org/extend/plugins/enhanced-text-widget/

Make your widgets more useful by increasing the type of text that can be displayed.

Flexo Archives

http://wordpress.org/extend/plugins/flexo-archives-widget/

Save space in your sidebar by displaying your archives using a collapsible display of years. This plugin was used on the Library of Congress blog.

jQuery Mega Menu

http://wordpress.org/extend/plugins/jquery-mega-menu/

If your navigation is too big to fit into short phrases, try using a mega menu!

One-Click Child Theme

http://wordpress.org/extend/plugins/one-click-child-theme/

If you do not have access to your website's server, you can use this plugin to help you make a child theme.

OpenBook Book Data

http://wordpress.org/extend/plugins/openbook-book-data/

Save staff time and automatically pull a book's cover, author, publication information, and so on from the Open Library's database.

WP Page Numbers

http://wordpress.org/extend/plugins/wp-page-numbers/

Controls the display of post navigation on the bottom of lists as numbers instead of using the words *next* and *previous*. This plugin was used on the Topeka & Shawnee County Public Library website.

WP-Table Reloaded

http://wordpress.org/extend/plugins/wp-table-reloaded/

Design tables for your data without writing a line of HTML. This plugin was used on the Scholarly Publishing @ MIT Libraries website.

Media

Audio Player

http://wordpress.org/extend/plugins/audio-player/

Share your podcasts with this simple mp3 player. This plugin was used on the Topeka & Shawnee County Public Library website.

Cropnote
http://wordpress.org/extend/plugins/cropnote/

Add annotations to your images using this plugin. It works in a similar manner to Flickr's image annotations.

SlideDeck 2 Lite Responsive Content Slider
http://wordpress.org/extend/plugins/slidedeck2/

It is easy to create content sliders with this plugin. Content can be pulled in automatically from a number of online social sharing sites such as Pinterest and YouTube. This plugin was used on the Lanier Theological Library website.

Smooth Slider
http://wordpress.org/extend/plugins/smooth-slider/

Pack a lot of content into a small space with an image slider with a variety of transition effects. This plugin was used on the Ask a Librarian Delaware website.

Video Embed & Thumbnail Generator
http://wordpress.org/extend/plugins/video-embed-thumbnail-generator/

By default, videos you upload to your self-hosted website show up as links. Use this plugin to make your videos appear within your post or page like a traditional embedded video.

WP Featured Content Slider
http://wordpress.org/extend/plugins/wp-featured-content-slider/

Show off your content using this slider, which packs a lot of punch in a small space. This plugin was used on the Topeka & Shawnee County Public Library website.

WP Photo Album Plus
http://wordpress.org/extend/plugins/wp-photo-album-plus/

Organize your images into albums instead of the default galleries.

Search Engine Optimization

All in One SEO Pack
http://wordpress.org/extend/plugins/all-in-one-seo-pack/

Prepare your website to be found by search engines with this optimization plugin. This plugin was used on the Ask a Librarian Delaware Staff website.

Yoast WordPress SEO

http://wordpress.org/extend/plugins/wordpress-seo/

Improve your site's rank in search engines with this sophisticated analysis plugin that checks for ways to improve your website. This plugin was used on the Topeka & Shawnee County Public Library website.

Social Networking

Achievements for BuddyPress

http://wordpress.org/extend/plugins/achievements/

Used in conjunction with BuddyPress to create an interactive and reward-driven social networking website. This plugin was used on the Learn@The Corkboard and Teen Summer Challenge websites.

BuddyPress

http://wordpress.org/extend/plugins/buddypress/

WordPress alone cannot deliver you a thriving social network, so enter BuddyPress, which empowers user engagement. This plugin was used on the Learn@The Corkboard and Teen Summer Challenge websites.

Digress.it

http://wordpress.org/extend/plugins/digressit/

Let users comment on the paragraph level of your text. This plugin was used on the New York Public Library's Candide 2.0 website.

Mingle Forum

http://wordpress.org/extend/plugins/mingle-forum/

WordPress can also give you the ability to host forums. This plugin was used on Darien Library's KidLibCamp unconference website.

Subscription Options

http://wordpress.org/extend/plugins/subscription-options/

Encourage patrons to have your content delivered to them by their preferred method: RSS, e-mail, Twitter, or Facebook. This plugin was used on the West Des Moines Library *Children's Blog*.

WP-PostRatings

http://wordpress.org/extend/plugins/wp-postratings/

Let users vote for their favorite content on your website! This plugin was used on the ReferencePoint website.

Teaching

BuddyPress Courseware

http://wordpress.org/extend/plugins/buddypress-courseware/

Turn BuddyPress into a class website with lectures, bibliography, assignments, scheduling options, and more!

Learninglog

http://wordpress.org/extend/plugins/learninglog/

For a simple student website, teachers can create learning logs for students to share and document their work.

CP Appointment Calendar.

http://wordpress.org/extend/plugins/cp-appointment-calendar/

Let WordPress handle appointment and meeting scheduling for you! Visitors receive a confirmation e-mails.

WP Teacher

http://wordpress.org/extend/plugins/wp-teacher/

Display a list of assignments and events on your website. Students can upload their documents on the assignment page.

Smallerik File Browser

http://wordpress.org/extend/plugins/smallerik-file-browser/

Students or patrons can access their own file repository on WordPress using this plugin.

Users

User Role Editor

http://wordpress.org/extend/plugins/user-role-editor/

If WordPress's default user roles are not to your liking, alter them!

WordPress Users

http://wordpress.org/extend/plugins/wordpress-users/

Show off your site's users!

Statistics

Google Analytics

http://wordpress.org/extend/plugins/google-analytics-for-wordpress/

How is your website doing? Google Analytics will tell you! This plugin was used on multiple library websites.

Jetpack

http://wordpress.org/extend/plugins/jetpack/

The all-in-one plugin that gives you statistics, a URL shortener, a spellchecker, and more. This plugin was used on Energy, Economics and the Environment: A Casebook Supplement Site.

W3 Total Cache.

http://wordpress.org/extend/plugins/w3-total-cache/

This plugin was used on the West Des Moines Library *Children's Blog*.

WP Accessibility

http://wordpress.org/extend/plugins/wp-accessibility/

Helps make your website more accessible for users with disabilities.

WP-DB-Backup

http://wordpress.org/extend/plugins/wp-db-backup/

Automate your site's database backup with this simple plugin; you can receive your backup in an e-mail, or it can backup to the server. You choose how often you want your backup to take place.

Index

3 1524 00637 7792